20 Formative Asse
Strategies that Work

This book provides teachers and school leaders with practical, effective, and proven assessment strategies that are immediately implementable in classrooms. You'll learn about 20 high-impact formative assessment strategies, with details on how they can be applied to a variety of content areas and grade levels, including Mathematics, Science, Language Arts, Social Studies, and various electives. In this accessible book, these experienced authors demonstrate the *how* and *why*, along with a framework for folding these new ideas into job-embedded professional development. *20 Formative Assessment Strategies that Work* provides the full toolkit for implementing, managing, and modifying these assessment strategies in your school and classrooms today.

Kate Wolfe Maxlow is Professional Learning Coordinator at Hampton City Schools in Hampton, Virginia, USA.

Karen L. Sanzo is Professor of Educational Leadership at Old Dominion University, USA.

Other Eye On Education Books Available from Routledge
(www.routledge.com/eyeoneducation)

20 Formative Assessment Strategies that Work

A Guide Across Content and Grade Levels

Kate Wolfe Maxlow
Karen L. Sanzo

Routledge
Taylor & Francis Group

NEW YORK AND LONDON

First published 2018
by Routledge
711 Third Avenue, New York, NY 10017

and by Routledge
2 Park Square, Milton Park, Abingdon, Oxon, OX14 4RN

Routledge is an imprint of the Taylor & Francis Group, an informa business

Library of Congress Cataloging-in-Publication Data
A catalog record for this book has been requested

ISBN: 978-1-138-04675-7 (hbk)
ISBN: 978-1-138-04676-4 (pbk)
ISBN: 978-1-315-17134-0 (ebk)

Typeset in Optima
by Apex CoVantage, LLC

Contents

Meet the Authors

Karen L. Sanzo is a Professor of Educational Leadership in the Darden College of Education at Old Dominion University. Prior to her work at Old Dominion, Sanzo served as a middle school mathematics teacher and an elementary school administrator in Virginia. She has also served as Principal Investigator for several national and state-level grants in the areas of school leadership, formative assessment, and STEM education. She also works with several educational organizations around leadership development initiatives and the integration of effective formative assessment leadership and instructional practices in schools.

Kate Wolfe Maxlow is the Professional Learning Coordinator at Hampton City Schools in Hampton, Virginia. Previously she has been an educational consultant on teacher evaluation, an instructional coach, and a third and fourth grade teacher. She earned her undergraduate degree in history from the University of Virginia, a Master's in Elementary Education from the College of William and Mary, and her endorsement in administration from the College of William and Mary. Her educational passion is creating systems that help students succeed through meaningful and engaging instruction.

Preface

We have had a chance throughout our careers to work with many PK–12 educators around instructional improvement and student achievement. During our classroom visits, professional development sessions, and other interactions with teachers and school leaders we have continually landed on one primary area that has an immediate, demonstrable impact on student success related to learning objectives. This is the effective use of formative assessments.

Effective instruction is not possible without the daily use of formative assessments—and not just "doing" a formative assessment. This means designing the formative assessment for the specific learning task and learning domain, collecting data from the assessments, analyzing data, and using the information gleaned from those data to make adjustments in instruction. This also includes intentional forward feedback (both during the lesson and as a follow-up post-lesson) designed to help students move toward successful understanding of learning intentions.

Thankfully, there are many different types of formative assessments teachers can use. The challenge, however, is while there are many types of formative assessments, there are very few examples of how to use the assessments in different content areas and in different grade levels, as well as few examples of how to use the formative assessment as part of an instructional cycle. Additionally, most examples of assessments that educators find are a title and a brief one-or-two-paragraph description of the assessment, as well as occasionally an example graphic. Usually there is little more than that, which makes it extremely difficult for teachers to effectively implement those assessments with fidelity. Instead, many teachers may use formative assessments in a less than ideal manner and not use the assessment data to make instructional improvements.

Our book provides teachers and school leaders with 20 high-impact formative assessments that are immediately useable during instruction. Additionally, we include details on the application of the assessments to a variety of content areas as well as a specific example for how to use each formative assessment within a broader formative data–based decision making cycle.

This book is a follow-up to *Formative Assessment Leadership: Identify, Plan, Apply, Assess, Refine*, by Sanzo, Myran, and Caggiano (2015). That book is a guide for school personnel engaged in a whole-school and/or whole-organization improvement process. The authors provide an overview of formative assessments, how to understand assessment within the context of a formative process, and the critical nature of using a formative data—based decision making assessment cycle at the school level. An important component of the 2015 text is the understanding the authors provide about the factors to improve learning:

1. Forward feedback

2. Active involvement of students in their own learning

3. Adjusting teaching to take into account the results of formative assessments

4. A recognition of the profound influence assessment has on engagement and self-efficacy (p. 18)

Additionally, that earlier text addresses specific aspects of the change process, which is integral for implementing any new initiative (which is germane to the current book, as we take an approach to exploring formative assessments that is fundamentally different from most overviews of formative assessments).

Structure of the Book

Within this book we share formative assessments that can be used within specific aspects of the formative data–based decision making cycle introduced by Sanzo and colleagues (2015). It is not necessary to have read the 2015 text to use this book. While the books are designed to dovetail with one another, these two texts dive into very different aspects of the cycle.

Our book provides guidance on how to use formative assessment strategies within the daily instructional process.

In order to provide an adequate grounding to the use of the assessments and the processes outlined for each of the 20 assessments, we first provide an overview of formative assessments (and the difference between summative assessments). That understanding is critical to being able to effectively use formative assessments as part of an overall instructional process. Additionally, this grounding provides teachers using this book within a school setting or another professional learning community to engage in dialogue through a common understanding of formative assessments. We share the formative data–based decision making cycle, providing descriptions of each part of the cycle and focusing on the aspects most germane to the instructional process.

Once we have provided background on formative assessments, we then provide 20 high-impact formative assessments you can immediately use in any instructional setting. We have grouped the strategies into five different categories: Arts, Collaborative, Movement, Select Response, and Supply Response. We provide a description for each assessment in classroom-friendly language and include the category of cognitive process dimension (the learning domain on Bloom's Taxonomy). Within each formative assessment strategy overview we also provide useful tips on how to manage the formative assessment the first time it is used, as well as for future iterations, how to use data for instructional change and student learning, and how to modify and differentiate the strategy for varied learners. We use a direct, no-nonsense approach in this book that allows teachers to quickly read through the assessment, decide if that assessment is best used within her or his instructional plan, and learn how to collect and use data. We provide example tasks by subject, and we also share an overview of how to use the assessment within a specific subject and grade level, which provides even more direction for teachers as to how to integrate the strategies into their own classrooms. Additionally, for each formative assessment category we provide a brief professional development plan for faculty.

eResources

Several of the formative assessment strategies in this book have an accompanying resource available online. Look out for the eResource logo next to the description of certain assessments. Resources can be downloaded, printed, used to copy/paste text, and/or manipulated to suit your individualized use. You can access these downloads by visiting the book product page on our website: www.routledge.com/products/9781138046764. Then click on the tab that reads "eResources" and then select the file(s) you need. The file(s) will download directly to your computer.

Tool

- eResource A: Sing It Rubric
- eResource B: Who/What Am I This Time?: Student Response Sheet
- eResource C: . . . And Scene! Rubric
- eResource D: Check In, Check Out Summary Sheet and Rubric
- eResource E: Learning Upgrade Chart for Students
- eResource F: Four Corners Summary Sheet
- eResource G: Graffiti Art Summary
- eResource H: Human Likert Scale Rubric
- eResource I: Question Hunt Summary Sheets

- eResource J: Generic Quick Rubric for Formative Assessment Strategies: Individual Students

- eResource K: Generic Quick Rubric for Formative Assessment Strategies: Student Groups

Introduction
Formatively Assessing Learning

Instruction can be truly effective only when paired with the use of formative assessments. Formative assessments provide real-time feedback to students and teachers about what has been learned, how to measure that learning against set learning targets or intentions, and then how to adjust (both student and teacher) to better meet the learning goal. On most days in any high-performing classroom you will see students who are deeply engaged in their own learning and being successful with the content and skills. Teachers in those types of classrooms use powerful formative assessment strategies that oftentimes seem effortless and may be difficult to tease out of the regular instructional time. In fact, it is those types of formative assessments in particular that are the most powerful. Those are integrated formatted assessments that are a part of the fabric of the instructional process.

There are many reasons why good teachers should always use formative assessment strategies during instruction. We agree with Otero's (2006) assertion that "formative assessment has broad application for K–12 students' emotional, intellectual, linguistic, and personal development" (p. 247). Good formative assessment practices will result in high student self-efficacy and student achievement. These types of strategies—the ones we outline in our book—also have the added benefit of high engagement for students and, therefore, can also benefit the overall climate of the classroom by minimizing or eliminating disruptive behaviors through active involvement of students in their own learning.

Formative Versus Summative

Formative assessments are not quarterly benchmarks. They are not quizzes each week or chapter tests (Black, 2003). There has been an unfortunate side effect of the "formative assessment boom." This is the codifying of certain assessment activities and calling them *formative assessments*, with these "formative assessments" resembling quizzes and benchmarks more than formative assessment strategies. We are not saying these types of assessments are inherently bad (although too-frequent assessments that are more formal in nature unnecessarily encumber instructional time, disrupt the natural flow of the learning environment, and typically do not involve the student in the actual formative assessment process), but these tend to sway more on the side of summative assessments rather than formative. The use of authentic formative assessments are instrumental to classrooms.

Also, there is perhaps a misunderstanding of formative assessment strategies. Many teachers say they are "doing" formative assessments. You may see "red, yellow, green" stop lights on students desks that indicate students need help or "got" the activity, or a sticky note placed on chart paper during an activity that measures level of understanding, or students using Twitter to "tweet" out answers in a rapid fashion. Those are useful and good strategies *if used correctly*. These are only *actual formative assessment strategies* when they are part of the instructional process and if the learners and teacher use those data to help improve learning and instruction. For example, simply asking students to complete Exit Tickets and hand them to a teacher while leaving the room is not useful if the teacher casually reads through them and then sets them aside (or even worse, just tosses them into the trash can) and never uses that information to impact instruction or tells the students the results of the Exit Tickets and how those results are being used. Without diving into data, using those data to make changes in instruction, and helping students understand their own learning in relation to the formative assessments, the strategies actually do not help at all.

The primary role of assessment in the classroom is to promote learning (Black & Wiliam, 2006). Effective use of formative assessments can result in marked improvements in student achievement (Hattie, 2009). Formative assessments allow teachers to understand student learning strengths and area for improvement, use internal and external motivating factors to help encourage student learning and engagement, and provide feedback both to the teachers as well as—and even more importantly in many instances—to students (Black & Wiliam, 1998).

Formative assessment is essentially "a process for teachers and students to be engaged in a continuous cycle of assessment and feedback" (Sanzo et al., 2015, p. 17). Further, "[f]ormative assessment differs from summative assessment primarily in that it is a developmental way of evaluating the progress towards a specified goal" (Sanzo et al., 2015, p. 17). Teachers can help students can measure themselves towards specific goals by incorporating the following three-question process into their instructional process (Sanzo et al., 2015).

1. Where am I going? (Goal setting)

2. How am I doing compared to my goal? (Self-assessment)

3. How am I progressing toward the goal? (Self-monitoring)

The Power of Feedback

Effective formative assessments strategies are grounded in the use of providing "forward feedback" to students. The aforementioned three questions are important to use as a part of that forward-feedback process. Teachers can help students learn better through goal setting, comparison of progress to those goals, and conversation about how to progress to those goals. Non-specific feedback does not provide the type of support and knowledge needed in order to allow students to make that goal comparison, as well as the information needed to progress towards the goals.

There is a difference between non-specific, evaluative feedback that does not help promote student understanding and forward feedback that helps students make changes in their own conceptions and understandings of a subject or skill in order to better learn (Sanzo et al., 2015). Non-specific feedback typically sounds or looks like "good job," "way to go," "you really got that one right," "you didn't quite get that answer," "pay attention," and "try harder next time." Of course, you can add many other phrases to the ones we just outlined. The point is that non-specific feedback does nothing to help your student understand why she or he made an error or why he or she was correct with a certain problem, task, or activity.

Forward feedback "provides information that students can use to adjust their performance as they work towards a learning goal" (Sanzo et al., 2015, p. 19). According to Ackerman, Dommeyer, and Gross (2017), "[w]hen instructors alert students to the strengths and weaknesses of their work, that feedback provides a means by which students may assess their own performance and make improvements in their future work" (p. 38).

Students are involved in a "feedback loop" that provides students a model for learning and structured guidance towards a learning intention (Roskos & Neuman, 2012).

Formative Data–Based Decision Making Cycle

The formative data–based decision making cycle can be used at the classroom level, as well as at the school level. We feel this is an easy to use/ easy to manage process, versus some that may involve more complicated steps and are more rigid in design. One of the hallmarks of the cycle is the ability to move throughout the steps in a back-and-forth, fluid process. It also follows the typical instructional outline.

"The suggested iterative cycle involves evaluating need and identifying existing information, development of an actionable plan, putting the plan into motion, assessing progress, and making refinements based on what was learned so far" (Sanzo et al., 2015, p. 42). We introduce the cycle here, as we use the cycle within our overall description of how to use the 20 high-impact formative assessment strategies (see Figure I.1). For the

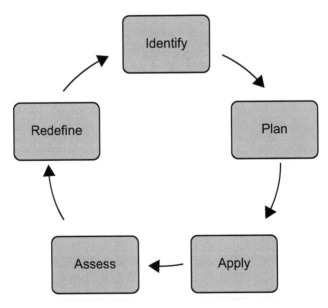

Figure I.1 The formative data–based decision making assessment cycle

purpose of this book and in order for you to situate the strategy descriptions within the cycle, we provide a brief overview of each step in the cycle. A more expansive description may be found in Sanzo et al. (2015).

Identify

In this step of the formative data–based decision making assessment cycle, teachers identify the focus for the unit, as well as the specific day within the unit for which the plan is being made (more nuanced daily planning components are done within the "Plan" step). Ideally this is done in grade level and/or content teams. One misunderstanding in this step and in the Plan step, however, is that only grade-alike or content-alike teachers should collaborate (Pre-Algebra teachers with other Pre-Algebra teachers, grade K with other grade K, 10th grade health teacher with other 10th grade health teachers). We advocate that while it is ideal for grade and content-alike teachers to plan together, that should not be the absolute in planning. Many schools only have one grade-level teacher or content teacher. There is much benefit in planning across grades and content, including vertical alignment, benefiting from differences in instructional views, and taking advantage of added expertise. Do not let a limited number of teachers within your own subject/grade area prevent you from working with others throughout the cycle.

At this step the teacher should look at any student learning errors and misconceptions that are typical for this unit and day. This is generally done at the macro level in this step, using school, grade, and content-level data. Teachers should be aware of typical learning challenges for the unit and lesson, those "typical" and consistent/persistent learning misconceptions that arise within the unit.

Plan

This step takes the teacher to the daily learning intention(s)/target(s) for the lesson. At this point if there is more than one teacher involved with the subject/grade level, we advocate for collaborative planning (and continue to advocate for cross-grade and content-level planning for those schools with smaller numbers of staff). Teachers can collectively unpack the learning standard, and develop learning intentions and student success criteria. These are important as students will use those as a measure of comparison for (1) where they are going; (2) how they are doing compared to the goal; and (3) how they are progressing toward the goal.

Apply

This step involves the teacher carrying out the plan and using the formative assessment strategy or strategies for the lesson. "An important part of the Apply step is built-in opportunities for teachers and instructional leaders to reflect on observed changes in student interactions in the classroom: Potential changes in engagement with the content, their classmates, and the teacher" (Sanzo et al., 2015, p. 43).

Assess

> The next step of the model provides the vital link to all the preceding steps by gathering empirical evidence of the impact of the evaluation of previous data, the identification of targeted areas of focus, and the associated planning and application of instructional and assessment strategies. During this step, teachers and instructional leaders are able to ascertain which aspects of their planning and implementation were effective, which showed promise, and which seemed to miss the mark.
>
> (Sanzo et al., 2015, p. 43)

Refine

At the classroom level, the Refine step involves the teacher recognizing where students are in terms of their own learning and the identified learning intentions. The teacher can refine her or his lesson for the next day (or during the instructional time) to differentiate based on learner needs, where to add additional learning support, and where she or he can provide extended learning opportunities for students successful with the learning target.

Formative Assessment Strategy Organization

Each of the 20 high-impact strategies described in this book follows the same organizational structure. We first introduce the overarching category and provide a description of the category, as well as research to support the category. We explain why the category works for instruction and provide some helpful tips to consider when using a formative assessment strategy from this category. At the end of the formative assessments within the specific category we also provide a brief professional development plan to help professional learning communities explore the category.

We use the following structure to introduce each high-impact formative assessment strategy.

Description: We provide a brief description of the strategy. The description is brief enough that you can "eyeball" the formative assessment strategy and decide if it is relevant to what you are working towards within your instructional plan.

Category of Cognitive Process Dimension: Using Anderson and Krathwohl's revision of Bloom's Taxonomy (Anderson et al., 2001), also known as *Bloom's Revised Taxonomy*, we present the level of cognitive domain the strategy best fits within. However, if there are additional applicable domains, we share possible approaches to working within those domains.

Bloom's Revised Taxonomy

Remember: Recognizing or recalling knowledge from memory. Remembering is when memory is used to produce or retrieve definitions, facts, or lists, or to recite previously learned information (Wilson, 2016, p. 2).

Understand: Constructing meaning from different types of functions, be they written or graphic messages, or performing activities such as interpreting, exemplifying, classifying, summarizing, inferring, comparing, or explaining (Wilson, 2016, p. 2).

Apply: Carrying out or using a procedure through executing, or implementing. Applying relates to or refers to situations where learned material is used through products like models, presentations, interviews, or simulations (Wilson, 2016, p. 2).

Analyze: Breaking materials or concepts into parts and determining how the parts relate to one another or how they interrelate, or how the parts relate to an overall structure or purpose. Mental actions included in this function are differentiating, organizing, and attributing, as well as being able to distinguish between the components or parts. When one is analyzing, one can illustrate this mental function by creating spreadsheets, surveys, charts, diagrams, or graphic representations (Wilson, 2016, pp. 2–3).

Evaluate: Making judgments based on criteria and standards through checking and critiquing. Critiques, recommendations, and reports are some of the products that can be created to demonstrate the processes of evaluation. In Bloom's Revised Taxonomy, evaluating comes before creating as it is often a necessary part of the precursory behavior before one creates something (Wilson, 2016, p. 3).

Create: Putting elements together to form a coherent or functional whole; reorganizing elements into a new pattern or structure through generating, planning, or producing. Creating requires users to put parts together in a new way, or synthesize parts into something new and different creating a new form or product. This process is the most difficult mental function in the revised taxonomy (Wilson, 2016, p. 3).

Learning Management: We provide brief helpful tips for teachers related to the strategy. These include procedural reviews and useful reminders about strategy use. This type of advice is very helpful for teachers new to the assessments we are sharing. As you use the strategies, we encourage you to make anecdotal notes in the book to give yourself additional bits of advice for future iterations of the strategy.

Using the Data Effectively: Effective use of the data is critical to fidelity of implementation for each strategy, as well as enhancing student learning. We provide advice on how to capture data and aspects of the data to consider.

Modifying and Differentiating the Strategy: There are many reasons why strategies should be modified and why you should differentiate, including age level of the learner, content level, and reading level, among other reasons. We provide tips on how to modify each strategy. As with learning management, we encourage you to write anecdotal notes to yourself about modification and differentiation as you use the strategies, too. We cannot anticipate all purposes for modification and differentiation within this book, but we provide a good starting point. This is an excellent area to connect with your colleagues around how they modify and differentiate the strategy to enhance student learning.

Examples by Subject: We believe all 20 of the high-impact formative assessment strategies presented in this book can be used throughout all grade levels and content areas. We share brief, practical examples of how the strategy can be used in the following content areas: English Language Arts, Mathematics, Science, Social Studies, World Languages, Music, Visual Arts, Health/Physical Education, Library/Media, and Career and Technical Education.

The Task from Start to Finish: We take you through the formative data–based decision making cycle to help with your planning process, briefly exploring the various steps by means of a practical, real-life example that is quick to read and easily understood in terms of how to use a particular content standard in your own work. As mentioned earlier, we have found this to be an area missing in most, if not all, of the formative assessment strategy resources currently available to educators.

Arts: Formative Assessment Strategies

Integrating the Arts into Formative Assessments

Have you ever said or heard any of the following from your colleagues?

- "We don't sing in my classroom. I can't sing and no one wants to hear that!"
- "I'm not an artist, so why would I do art in my classroom?"
- "I'm teaching Math (or Science or Library), not Fine Arts. Why would I have my kids sing or draw?"
- "All that arts integration stuff sounds great, but we don't have time for that with our packed curriculum."

If you have said or heard either of the first two, you are not alone. Studies have found that teachers are often reluctant to use the arts in their classrooms if they feel that their own artistic abilities are not up to par (Garvis & Pendergast, 2010; Oreck, 2004). We have great news, though: this chapter will show you how to easily integrate arts-related formative assessment tasks that require little to no training or natural artistic talent on your part! Not only can arts integration have a positive impact on your students' learning and achievement, it might even help you reach students who struggle to learn through what many consider more "traditional" methods.

Why Music Integration Works

There exists a common myth that in order to increase anyone's IQ, all a person has to do is listen to more Mozart. This idea came from a 1993 paper published in the journal *Nature*, in which the researchers found that having participants listen to a Mozart sonata improved their scores on spatial reasoning tests; unfortunately, subsequent studies have not yielded the same results (Johnson, 2013).

It turns out, however, that music *can* have a large impact on other areas that impact student success in the classroom. There is more and more evidence, for instance, supporting the link between exposure to music and language development (Asaridou & McQueen, 2013, McMullen & Saffran, 2004; Patel, 2003). Preschool students who are able to match a drumbeat are more likely to have stronger prereading skills; as Krause and Anderson (2015) point out, the "accurate temporal processing" that can be heightened by exposure to music is also part of foundational skills for reading.

Perhaps one of the greatest impacts of music on student achievement concerns the area of memory. If you have ever had a song "stuck in your head," then you already know the powerful effect music can have on memory. In research settings, music has been shown repeatedly to help participants memorize multiplication tables, phone numbers, random numbers, and much more (Silverman, 2010). Especially when learning unfamiliar material, music can act as a "structural prompt": we connect information with a particular rhythm and pitch that occur in a particular order (also known as a melody), so that we can recall information in a particular order based on our memorization of the melody itself (Silverman, 2010). In this way, music can be a powerful mnemonic device.

Why Visual Arts Integration Works

Have you ever caught yourself reading every word on a page but realizing you did not pay attention to a single word that you read? Or maybe you have taught a student who was a perfect "word-caller," who could easily pronounce each word on the page, but could not understand anything happening in the text? In these cases, the brain "reads" the words but fails to process or make meaning of what is being said, and this is a frequent barrier to comprehension.

Enter the Visual Arts as a potentially powerful solution. One of the common reasons people struggle with reading is their inability to visualize what is happening in a particular passage of text, leading to decreased comprehension. Purposefully building in tasks that require students to stop, visualize, and create a piece of art that represents their visualization has been shown to increase comprehension (Wilhelm, 1995), as well as being an engaging technique for students.

Why Drama Integration Works

There are three parts of the brain involved in making and retrieving memories: the amygdala, which processes emotions tied to the memory; the hippocampus, which determines where and how the memory will be stored; and the frontal cortex, which processes the individual memory as part of a whole narrative or framework (Armstrong, 2008). Infusing tasks that use dramatic acting into our lessons is one very strong method for activating all these sections of the brain.

For instance, when students perform, they automatically associate the academic information with the emotions they portray (not to mention the emotions that students themselves feel while doing the acting). The hippocampus is often engaged through repetition or reinforcement of the material; having students act out even a short scene multiple times engages this area of the brain. Lastly, having students put content information into the context of a short scene helps them use their frontal cortex to develop the narrative or framework.

Tips for Using Arts Tasks for Formative Assessment

- Because the arts can have such a powerful impact on student memory, the teacher should check in with students frequently while they create a work, and provide immediate feedback for any misconceptions to avoid students retaining incorrect information.

- Students who are not used to these types of tasks, especially older students, may be reluctant to engage in them at first, or worry the tasks are not "serious" academic pursuits. In this case, it may be helpful for the teacher to share some of the research regarding why and how these tasks can impact learning and memory retention with students.

● Teachers should strongly consider how much time they want to allot to a particular Arts task, and stick to it as much as possible; given the engaging nature of these activities, it can be easy to let an entire class period slip away in creating a perfect drawing or song. The teacher should help students remain focused on the academic objectives for the task by explaining that these particular tasks are meant to be tools to engage students and see what they know.

Postcard Summaries

Description

This activity allows students to create "postcards" of their learning. This is a fun, creative opportunity for students to draw a picture of their learning on one side of a "postcard" and provide a summary to a person (their post-card message) on the other side. Teachers are able to formatively assess students both through pictorial representation and a brief summary of learning.

This activity works best after a chunk of learning in order to have students summarize what they have learned (e.g., at the end of a lesson or at a hinge-point in the lesson). It can be used before having students move on to independent work or at the end of the lesson.

Give students a large notecard or half sheet of paper. Show them an example of a postcard. This is especially helpful and important when introducing this type of formative assessment to your students for the first time. On the front of the postcard there is usually a picture that "sums up" the place, and on the back there is room to write just one or two sentences sharing the main highlights or takeaways from the sender's trip. Explain to students that they are going to make a "postcard" of their learning.

On the front, they should create a quick drawing that "sums up" their learning. On the back, they should choose a person to "write home to," and write one or two sentences that share the main highlights or takeaways from their learning that day.

Category of Cognitive Process Dimension

It might be tempting to put this under the Create level because students are drawing pictures, but the thrust of the activity is not to create a new product as much as to use the drawing to demonstrate understanding. Therefore, this activity works best for assessing the Remember and Understand levels, although with some creativity in what students are asked to depict, it could be used for Application.

This activity probably would not give students enough time or space to properly Analyze or Evaluate, though it could be used to check for understanding of basic concepts before students move on to higher-level activities.

 ## Learning Management

It can be helpful to give students 60–90 seconds of "brainstorm" time to turn and talk to a partner before they begin drawing. This can help to solidify their ideas and help make their efforts directed and efficient.

Students might be inclined to spend a long time on their drawings. It can be helpful the first few times you use this formative assessment to give them a time limit for the drawing (three to five minutes) and then tell them when to move on to their highlights or takeaways (three to five minutes).

 ## Using the Data Effectively

Information can be gleaned both from what the students choose to depict and what they say about it. For instance, if a student is asked to draw George Washington's greatest achievement and they choose to draw our first president cutting down a cherry tree, that shows a serious misconception that needs to be corrected. Likewise, if the student draws George Washington being unanimously elected but explains that he was our second president, that also points to a misconception.

Teachers can then use the data to determine who needs to continue working with concepts and who is ready to move on, either to the next topic or to a higher-level activity.

Modifying and Differentiating the Strategy

For students who are not strong writers, you can simply have them draw the picture and then orally explain what they would write.

Students who are not strong artists can use collages (with stickers or cut-outs from magazines, for instance). In the case of very technical concepts, and especially with younger students, it might be easier to give students a blank diagram as their front picture. The teacher can also give students more direction regarding the picture, such as, "Draw three inclined surfaces that a block might roll down and rate each from fastest to slowest."

You can assign the "friend" to whom students will be writing, and then have them "deliver" the postcard and provide each other with peer feedback.

Examples by Subject

English Language Arts

Students can sum up any books they read (this is a great activity for independent reading groups as well as whole group) or more content-based lessons (e.g., idioms, fact versus opinion, figurative language, etc.).

Mathematics

Students can use the front to draw a mathematical representation of a problem or depict a real-life scenario in which they would use their learning. For example, during a lesson on area, the student might draw a garden and its measurements, then on the back, explain how to find the area.

Science

Students can use the front to show their understanding of a concept from either a teacher-guided lesson or an inquiry lesson. For instance, after having students experiment with friction by rolling a wooden or plastic block down different types of surfaces, students can draw a picture of the various surfaces and on the back explain why the marble rolls faster on some than others. Students can also draw pictures of what they saw in microscopes or diagrams of plants or animals.

Social Studies

This works especially well for events or concepts for which students can draw a depiction of their understandings. If the lesson is on a particular person, it is recommended the teacher require students to draw the person's major accomplishment, rather than just a portrait of the person.

World Languages

Students can draw examples of real-life interactions (such as two people greeting each other, or a person asking for directions) or examples of nouns (e.g., foods found in Francophone countries) or verbs (e.g., a person running). On the back, they can practice writing a sentence or more in the appropriate world language using the appropriate level of vocabulary and grammar.

Music

Students can use the front to draw musical symbols, then explain their meanings on the back, or use the postcard more abstractly to draw and describe how playing a piece of music makes them feel.

Visual Arts

A teacher can have students do a quick drawing of the concept for the day (such as line or perspective), their favorite piece of work by a particular artist, or an illustration for how to complete a particular action in a graphic design program.

Health/Physical Education

A student might draw ways to increase core strength, an example of a student assertively declining a risky action, or a particular rule for the sport being studied.

Library/Media

Students can draw various resources and then explain on the back what kind of information they usually contain, or use the postcard to sum up their research on a given subject.

Career and Technical Education

Students can draw a real-life example of a business strategy, how to successfully complete a nursing technique, or a car part and its role in making the car run.

The Task from Start to Finish

Identify

Mateo Molina teaches high school Earth Science. He is beginning a unit on Geology/Plate Tectonics.

Plan

Mateo reviews the Next Generation Science Standards for this standard:

HS-ESS1–5. Evaluate evidence of the past and current movements of continental and oceanic crust and the theory of plate tectonics to explain the ages of crustal rocks. [Clarification Statement: Emphasis is on the ability of plate tectonics to explain the ages of crustal rocks. Examples include evidence of the ages of oceanic crust increasing with distance from mid-ocean ridges (a result of plate spreading) and the ages of North American continental crust decreasing with distance away from a central ancient core of the continental plate (a result of past plate interactions).]

Phrase	Cognitive Process Dimension Category	Reasoning
Evaluate evidence of the past and current movements of continental and oceanic crust and the theory of plate tectonics to explain the ages of crustal rocks.	Evaluate	While the thrust of this standard is that students can explain the ages of crustal rocks, they should be able to do so evaluating the evidence of past and current movements of continental and oceanic crust and the theory of plate tectonics.

While this particular standard is at the Evaluate level, Mateo knows that in order to be able to evaluate evidence using the theory of plate tectonics to explain the ages of crustal rocks, his students must first understand the theory of plate tectonics. He therefore wants to formatively assess their understanding before moving on.

Apply

Mateo does a lesson with students specifically on the theory of plate tectonics. Afterwards, he asks students to do a Postcard Summary, which he has had them do before. He tells students they can either draw their picture first or write their sentences, but they have three minutes to complete each side. He sets a timer for three minutes and when it goes off, tells students to flip their papers. Mateo then has students share their Postcard Summary with a shoulder partner for two minutes (one minute each to share) and gives students another two minutes to refine either their pictures or their sentences.

Assess

Mateo reviews each student's postcard. In a corner of each postcard, he writes down notes about the major concepts that the student misunderstood; see Figures 1.1 and 1.2 for example postcards. The next day, during

divergent
Pangea = super continent
subduction
convergent
transform

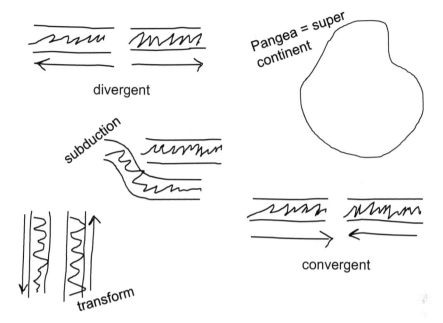

Figure 1.1 Example of student postcard drawing that shows understanding of the three major ways that plates move

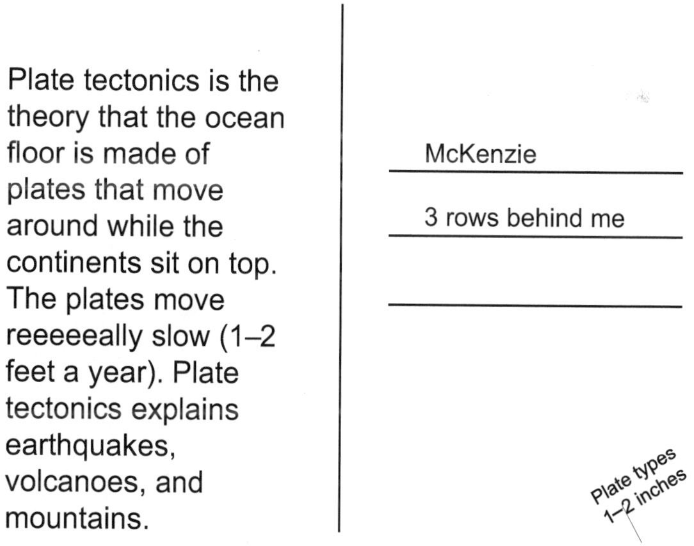

Plate tectonics is the theory that the ocean floor is made of plates that move around while the continents sit on top. The plates move reeeeeally slow (1–2 feet a year). Plate tectonics explains earthquakes, volcanoes, and mountains.
McKenzie
3 rows behind me
Plate types
1–2 inches

Figure 1.2 This student has a general misunderstanding about the types of plates and how far plates move each year

a review activity, he meets with each student to quickly conference about these misunderstandings.

He notices that 17 of 27 students seem to be confused about the different types of plates. He therefore quickly reviews this with the whole class. After these review sessions, he feels ready to move on to the higher-level activities in which students examine evidence.

Refine

Mateo realizes it was difficult to gauge what some students knew because their drawings and sentences were too vague. While he does meet with these students to review and informally assess their understanding, he decides that next time he will post major vocabulary words that students must include in either their drawings or their descriptions.

2 | Sculpt It

Description

All the tactile learners in class will love being able to do a very hands-on formative assessment. Teachers can use inexpensive modeling dough to have students create a sculpture of the main idea of the topic. This formative assessment works best when students can explain their thinking either orally or in writing.

Category of Cognitive Process Dimension

While the activity itself is at the Create level, it works well for almost any level of standard. For upper levels like Apply, Analyze, and Evaluate, the teacher might need to demonstrate to students how to create a sculpture that expresses those levels of thinking.

Learning Management

The teacher will want to establish and review procedures for using the modeling dough in the classroom, including:

- Do not mix colors.
- Ensure that the dough is stored properly.
- Keep the dough on the desks/tables and clean up any dough on the floor immediately.
- If the classroom is carpeted, ensure some sort of plastic covering protects the floor before the students work.

Using the Data Effectively

The teacher should review students' conceptual understandings about main ideas by either listening to their oral explanations or reading their written explanations and reviewing with individual students, or the group, as necessary.

 # Modifying and Differentiating the Strategy

Do not think this activity is limited to younger students! Believe it or not, even high school students have fun with this activity. It works well for students who are not strong writers, as well as English Language Learners. It can also help strengthen fine motor coordination.

 # Examples by Subject

English Language Arts

Students can sculpt elements from stories, such as characters, settings, the climax, etc.

Mathematics

This is a great way to help students work through word problems concretely. For instance, they could sculpt a 3 × 3 square and cube to demonstrate their understanding of exponents and review how squaring and cubing are similar and different.

Science

Students can use sculpture to demonstrate their knowledge, such as by sculpting cells, cycles, circuits, etc.

Social Studies

This task can be used for several subjects in Social Studies, from Geography (sculpting the shape or topography of a location) to History (sculpting key events) to civics (Sculpting legislative processes) and more.

World Languages

The teacher can have students demonstrate their knowledge of various cultures, or elements of stories read in the world language being studied.

Music

Students can sculpt how songs make them feel, instruments in various categories, and notes from what they consider the "most challenging" section of their performed music.

Visual Arts

Sculpture certainly is a major part of the Visual Arts, so it works very naturally in this subject area. Students can sculpt their understanding of shapes, lines, etc., both in general and in specific works of art.

Health/Physical Education

Types of exercises to improve health, nutritious meals, and bodily systems can all be sculpted.

Library/Media

Students can sculpt principles of digital citizenship, steps in the inquiry process, or their main understandings after conducting research on a topic.

Career and Technical Education

Automotive parts and systems, economic principles, and healthcare techniques can all be sculpted.

The Task from Start to Finish

Identify

Michael DiRollo is a third-grade teacher planning a lesson for reading for his unit on Fables, Folktales, and Myths Around the World. He especially wants to know whether his students understand the moral of the stories they read during this unit.

Plan

Michael looks up the Common Core Standards for English Language Arts, Reading: Literature and unpacks the following standard:

CCSS.ELA-LITERACY.RL.3.2.   Recount stories, including fables, folktales, and myths from diverse cultures; determine the central message, lesson, or moral and explain how it is conveyed through key details in the text.

Phrase	Cognitive Process Dimension Category	Reasoning
Recount stories, including fables, folktales, and myths from diverse cultures; determine the central message, lesson, or moral and explain how it is conveyed through key details in the text.	Understand	Because students are retelling the stories in their own words, they are working at the Understand level. Similarly, being able to determine the central message, lesson, or moral demonstrates comprehension of the text, which would be the Understand level.

Apply

After reading the fable "The Town Mouse and the Country Mouse" with students in a small group and demonstrating to students how to sculpt the moral of the story, Michael gives his group the leveled copy of the fable "The Ant and the Grasshopper" to read on their own. He gives each student two small tubs of modeling clay and asks them to sculpt the moral of that story. He then asks each student to explain their sculpture to the group while he jots down data on both their understanding of the moral and the explanation.

Assess

Michael keeps the following chart for this particular small group:

Correct moral, clear explanation	Correct moral, vague explanation	Incorrect moral, clear explanation	Incorrect moral, vague explanation
Fiona Jaelynn	Gabriel Isis Laura	Joshua	N/A

For this group, Michael realizes the majority of the students (five of six) understand how to identify the moral of the fable. Only two students were able to provide clear explanations for how they knew that was the moral, however, using evidence from the text. Michael therefore decides he needs to do more modeling with this group on how to use evidence from the text to justify their explanations of the moral. He also decides to keep Joshua behind for a few minutes after dismissing the rest of the group to work with him one-on-one on determining the moral.

Refine

Michael's students enjoy sculpting the moral of the story. Michael determines that next time he will also demonstrate to them how to write down their explanations on a notecard.

3 | Sing It

Description

Teachers have long known the value in helping students remember information by teaching them songs. This activity has students create a song to demonstrate their understanding.

While the teacher can allow students to compose their own melodies, it is suggested the teacher also give students several common melody options, such as "Row Your Boat," "America the Beautiful," or "Jingle Bells." Songs should be short, and students should perform them for one another.

It is also helpful if the teacher provides students with a list of vocabulary words that need to be included in the song to help give students an idea of where to start, and to make sure they hit key information.

With the teacher's permission, students can also use other melodies.

Category of Cognitive Process Dimension

The activity itself is at the Create level, but works especially well with standards at the Remember and Understand level. It can be used with standards at higher levels with some creativity on the teacher's part. For songs at the Evaluate level, it might be helpful to listen to protest songs or similar songs with students beforehand to help them understand how to work at higher levels.

Learning Management

The teacher will want to discuss with students beforehand that singing ability is not the key point of the lesson, and encourage a climate of trust and respect so students are not overly self-conscious. Students can also work in groups or have "backup" singers to lessen stage fright. In some cases, the teacher might also elect to sing the song for the class after the student has written it.

Using the Data Effectively

The teacher should use student songs to determine misconceptions, areas of strengths, and areas of weakness for individual students and the class as a whole.

Modifying and Differentiating the Strategy

For very young students it might be helpful to work with them in small groups to help them understand the process. For students unfamiliar with traditional American songs, the teacher may want to provide examples of the song or allow students to use songs from their native cultures.

Examples by Subject

English Language Arts

Students summarize the book *The Grapes of Wrath*.

Mathematics

Students create a song to outline the steps for solving multi-step mathematics problems.

Science

Students design a song that details the stages of the rock cycle.

Social Studies

Students research a Latin American country and create a song that explains the country's geographic features, resources, and population.

World Languages

Students write a call-and-response song in which they use common phrases and answers.

Music

Students can write a song with vocabulary terms and their definitions.

Visual Arts

Students can look at pieces from various periods in art and write songs about their major characteristics.

Health/Physical Education

Students can write songs about body systems and facts about them.

Library/Media

Students can create songs about how to use the inquiry method to design and conduct research projects.

Career and Technical Education

Students can write a song explaining how to conduct CPR or administer first aid.

The Task from Start to Finish

Identify

Xiomara Garcia is a Library/Media specialist in a middle school that serves sixth through eighth grades. She is working with the seventh graders on a three-day unit on Digital Citizenship and Citing Sources in collaboration with their English classes.

Plan

Xiomara looks up the Standards for the 21st-Century Learner from the American Association of School Librarians and unpacks the following:

1.3.1   Respect copyright/intellectual property rights of creators and producers.

Phrase	Cognitive Process Dimension Category	Reasoning
Respect copyright/ intellectual property rights of creators and producers.	Apply	In order to fully respect the copyright/intellectual property, students must apply their knowledge of these concepts when researching.

Xiomara teaches a lesson on how to use copyrighted material and respect intellectual property when doing research. During the lesson, students take notes in a graphic organizer. Afterward, Xiomara wants to see if students understand the main concept, so she decides to use the Sing It task.

Apply

Xiomara explains the Sing It task to students, then gives them five song melodies from which to choose. She uses melodies from current popular songs that she knows her students will have heard and tells them they only have to write a verse and a chorus and their lyrics don't have to rhyme. She then gives students an example (with the provision that they cannot use that song).

Students are given the option of working either individually or in groups of up to three, and are told they only have 10 minutes to prepare their song, so they should keep it simple—about 30 seconds.

At the end of 10 minutes, she has students perform for one another. They do silent cheers for one another, and give each other written feedback using "I like" (in which they write a specific thing that they liked) and "I wonder" (in which they describe something that the songwriter(s) could maybe do to improve their song). Xiomara reads the "I likes" and "I wonders" before giving them to the group.

Assess

Xiomara rates the groups using the following scale like so:

Song provides detailed understanding with correct content	Song is either somewhat vague or contains minimal misconceptions	Song is either very vague or contains many misunderstandings
Allegra & Cho Gretel & Wynn Tinesha & Whitney Bentley, Graeme, & Nick Evie Asia & Alexandra	Quentin Miles & Ricky Miller & McKenzie	Olivia & Lola Chris & Dawson

The next day, Xiomara allows the students in the first column to begin working on their research task immediately, but checks in with students in the other two columns first to revisit the previous day's lesson and make sure they understand how to properly cite sources.

Refine

Xiomara's students enjoyed the lesson. She decides to allow students to revisit their songs at the beginning of the third day to see if they would update them based on their learning from the second day.

Who/What Am I This Time?

Description

This is a fun formative assessment activity that gives students a chance to "act out" some aspect of the current instructional unit. Students are given notecards with a person or concept from the current unit, but the notecard is either secured or held so that while everyone else can see it, the student him- or herself cannot. Other students must then act out the notecard without saying the word on the card.

Category of Cognitive Process Dimension

This activity works best for the Remember, Understand, and Apply levels.

Learning Management

One easy way to keep students from seeing their notecards is to use lanyards and name badge holders, which can often be bought in bulk online. The teacher can then quickly stick the notecard with the name or concept into each lanyard and have students wear it backwards so the lanyard hangs down their backs. This way, everyone else can easily see the notecard, but the student cannot.

While you can have students do this one at a time in front of the whole class or in a small group, it works well to have students walk around and use a Hand Up–Pair Up to have them interact. Students walk around the room until the teacher says to stop (or turns off music or flicks lights on and off) and then raise their hands. They high-five someone near them (who will be her or his partner) and then put their hands down to acknowledge they have a pair. This way, students can easily see who else still needs a partner.

The teacher will need to demonstrate to students how to act out the person or concept and potentially how to move around the classroom.

Using the Data Effectively

The teacher will want to informally observe students and collect information through observation. For older students, having them write down what word/concept they think they are based on their classmates' words/actions can help the teacher to determine who knows what and why.

Modifying and Differentiating the Strategy

The teacher can allow students to speak (easier) or require them to act out their words/concepts (harder). For younger students, the teacher can provide pictures along with, or instead of, words.

Examples by Subject

English Language Arts

Words/concepts can include vocabulary words, characters, scenes from stories, and elements of nonfiction.

Mathematics

Students can be given a notecard with a formula and other students have to act out where in real life it might be used. Students can also be given vocabulary words or steps in the problem-solving process.

Science

Vocabulary words, steps in the process of scientific investigations, cycles and processes, and historical scientific discoveries can all be used for this assessment activity.

Social Studies

Students can be given cards with people, places, dates, concepts, and events.

World Languages

This is a great activity to help test students' knowledge of vocabulary words in the language being studied.

Music

Instruments, musical terms, musical time periods, and genres work well for this activity.

Visual Arts

Processes for creating art, elements of art and design, artists, famous works of art, and art time periods can all be used.

Health/Physical Education

Ideas include muscle groups, types of exercises, rules for games, health vocabulary, and concepts.

Library/Media

A Library/Media specialist might use this to assess literacy genres, steps in the inquiry process, or research methodologies.

Career and Technical Education

ROTC drill procedures, Economics terms, healthcare procedures and terms, computer parts, and software titles can all be used with this activity.

The Task from Start to Finish

Identify

Carl Lo teaches U.S. History for seventh grade students. He is finishing a unit on the era leading up to the U.S. Civil War and wants to assess what students know while helping them review.

Plan

Carl decides to use the Who/What Am I This Time? task with his students. He unpacks the National Curriculum Standards for Social Studies and uses the following standard for the activity:

Theme 5:   Individuals, Groups, and Institutions: Learners will be able to understand examples of tensions between belief systems and governmental actions and policies.

Phrase	Cognitive Process Dimension Category	Reasoning
Learners will be able to understand examples of tensions between belief systems and governmental actions and policies.	Understand	Carl teaches students how individuals' and groups' belief systems differed with the government and laws in the era leading up to the Civil War. He ensures that students are able to explain in their own words.

Apply

Carl pulls out several people, places, and events from the curriculum students need to know for their assessment, such as Frederick Douglass, John

36

Brown, the Seneca Falls Convention, and Uncle Tom's Cabin. He uses name badges on lanyards and puts a note card with an important term on them. He then gives each student one lanyard to wear around their necks backward so they cannot see what term they have but everyone else can. He has 29 students and 15 terms, so he simply repeats some of the terms on the note cards, meaning that two students have Frederick Douglass, two students have John Brown, and so on.

He also gives students a list of the potential terms and gives them five minutes before the actual activity to quickly review the terms using their notes and textbooks. He lets students know they will not be able to talk during the activity and they will have to act everything out just like in charades. Carl tells them to use the five minutes to think about what actions they might use to depict the terms.

Carl then has students move around the classroom and has students do a Hand Up–Pair Up four times to interact with others student in order to determine the term they have on their backs.

At the end, he goes around the classroom and has students guess who or what they had, and then asks them to turn around their lanyard and see if they are correct. He then has students fill out an Exit Ticket that he can use to evaluate their understanding.

Assess

Carl reviews the Exit Tickets and makes notes about what to review with students. Here are two example Exit Tickets completed by students:

Kirsten				
Who/what did you think you had?	Who/what did you have?	What evidence from your peers was most on-point?	What evidence from your peers was most misleading?	What's one thing you wish your peers had done to help you guess?
Harriet Beecher Stowe	Harriet Beecher Stowe	Andie did the sign for book. Marcus pretended to be a slave running away.	Joseph pretended to be fighting, which made me wonder if I had John Brown or Nat Turner.	I thought Andie's and Marcus's hints were perfect.

Manley				
Who/what did you think you had?	Who/what did you have?	What evidence from your peers was most on-point?	What evidence from your peers was most misleading?	What's one thing you wish your peers had done to help you guess?
Nat Turner	John Brown	Fighting	I couldn't tell that they were fighting.	I don't know.

From these two examples, Carl can tell that Kirsten has a decently firm understanding about three of the terms (Harriet Beecher Stowe, John Brown, and Nat Turner). He can also see that Manley does not provide much information and seems confused about the differences between Nat Turner and John Brown, so Carl makes a note to himself to check in with Manley before the assessment and provide him with extra review practice.

Refine

Carl decides that next time he will give students five extra minutes to do a Think-Pair-Share while reviewing the terms beforehand so they can give each other ideas.

Professional Development Plan
Arts Tasks

Step 1

Read the chapter in advance of meeting as a group. Ask teachers in advance of coming to the professional development session to take three pictures with their smartphones that help describe the way they feel when a student "gets" the lesson they are teaching. Ask them to bring their phones—or printouts of the pictures—to the professional development activity.

Step 2

In a face-to-face professional development session that is approximately one hour in length:

- Pair the teachers up or place them in groups of three.
- Ask the teachers to share each of their pictures and describe why they chose the pictures.

After everyone has had a turn discuss why this is an Arts strategy, and in particular a modified version of the Postcard Summary. Rather than drawing a picture, an alternative approach to drawing was used (the smartphone), which could therefore be used by students who do not feel comfortable drawing. This could also use an alternative modality such as a tablet PC. Additionally, rather than a written summary, teachers verbally explained their own learning and feelings related to students learning a lesson.

- Give participants this task: "Use at least one of the Arts formative assessment techniques in your class over the next week and be ready to discuss how it went." Optional: require participants to try out two of the tasks.

◼ Step 3

Conduct walkthroughs as staff implement the arts formative assessment strategies over the next week. Consider collaborative walkthroughs as well as individual peer walkthroughs.

◼ Step 4

In a follow-up face-to-face professional development session approximately one hour in length:

- Place signs in three of the corners of the room that read: Postcard Summaries, Sculpt It, and Sing It.

Have appropriate materials for each of the strategies in each corner connected with the strategy. For example, for Sculpt It have modeling clay and for Postcard Summaries have sheets of paper and markers.

Ask teachers to choose one of the corners and then use that formative assessment strategy to summarize their experiences with the arts formative assessment strategies they used over the last two weeks. Give them a set amount of time to complete the strategy—about 10 to 15 minutes. Allow teachers to have conversations within their corners (and prompt conversation if the teachers are quiet).

Put participants in groups of four (either heterogeneous or with like grade levels/subject areas). Have each group discuss the following reflection questions:

- What task did you try? What worked well? What might you do differently next time?
- What instructional decisions did you make based on the task?
- How will you use this professional development to make a change in your practice that positively impacts your students and their achievement?

Collaborative: Formative Assessment Strategies
Integrating Collaboration into Formative Assessments

Student collaboration can range from very formal, semi-permanent structures to less formal and more ad hoc. The tasks suggested by this book tend to be the latter in scope, allowing you flexibility to insert the strategies easily into units or lessons as quick methods to see what students know.

 ## Effects on Academics

Student collaborative, or cooperative, learning has a long history of positively impacting student achievement. Researchers tend to look at three types of learning structures: collaborative/cooperative (in which students work together to reach a goal), competitive (in which students compete against each other to reach a goal), and individualistic (in which students work alone to reach a goal). What they generally find is that collaborative learning tends to promote higher achievement than competitive or individualistic learning. Moreover, students who engage in collaborative learning also tend to spend more time on-task and work harder to achieve success (Johnson & Johnson, n.d.).

Interestingly, the effects of collaboration on student achievement increase as students age (Hattie, 2009). This means that, in opposition to what some may think, we need to ensure more, rather than less, collaboration as students move through school.

Several researchers have noted, however, that several elements should be in place in order to reap the benefits of student collaboration. First and foremost the teachers needs to build in measures of both group and individual accountability to ensure everyone contributes (Stevens & Slavin, 1990); much of the impact from collaboration comes from the interplay of ideas and skills of the individuals. The teacher should also be prepared to teach appropriate group interactions to students, such as active listening, asking clarifying questions, explaining opinions, and encouraging each other (Slavin, 2014).

We feel that because of the critical nature of collaboration and how significant the potential is for the strategy to impact student achievement, teachers need to work collectively to learn about the Collaborative strategies. In effect, teachers collaborating around the Collaborative strategies can have a positive, compounding effect on the fidelity of implementation for these strategies. We encourage you to discuss the various strategies as a group, collect data as you implement these strategies, and debrief post-strategy to engage in a formative assessment "lesson study" to better understand how the strategy worked.

Effects on Non-Academic Areas

The benefits of working with peers to accomplish a goal go beyond academics, though. Collaborative work has been shown to increase motivation, self-esteem, and overall academic engagement, and decrease loneliness (Pitler, Hubbell, & Kuhn, 2012). When done well, the positive interactions that can come from student collaboration can lead to fewer absences and lower dropout rates (Johnson & Johnson, 2009). Furthermore, there is evidence that students who engage in more collaborative structures in school tend to be more mature in both their cognitive reasoning and moral decision making (Johnson & Johnson, n.d.).

Tips for Using Collaborative Tasks for Formative Assessment

- If either the teacher or the students are new to collaborative work you should "start small." Take just one portion of a lesson and insert a quick activity, such as the Group Graphic Organizers. More formal group work, like . . . And Scene! or Check In, Check Out, and more long-term tasks, such as Learning Upgrade Charts, will work better once students are comfortable working with others and group work norms have been established.

- Make sure you always build individual accountability into any group-work task. Several of the tasks in the following four assessments describe how to do just that (such as writing with different color markers in the Group Graphic Organizers, or calling on individual students during scene debriefs in . . . And Scene!). These are essential pieces; resist the urge to remove individual accountability in an effort to streamline a lesson.

- Most feedback students receive is from other students (Nuthall, 2007); we therefore need to ensure we structure this learning for quality feedback and positive interactions (Hattie, 2009). Model these conversations for your students and allow them opportunities to practice.

- Group goals can help students use collaborative time productively, and goals that one student cannot complete alone work best (Slavin, 2014). Make sure to state goals clearly for students and explain how they will work together to reach them.

Assessment

...And Scene!

Description

Teachers often have students create skits to demonstrate their learning; students perform their skits while the rest of the class watches passively. This task is different because students are assessed during their time as audience members as well as when performing.

The teacher will want to divide students into groups with three or four students per group. Depending on the number of groups, the teacher will choose that many vocabulary words or concepts plus two more. For instance, in a classroom of 23 students, the teacher might break up students into seven groups; in that case, the teacher will need nine concepts or terms for the activity. The teacher will need to write each word or concept on a separate note card (in our example, the teacher will therefore need nine notecards).

While the teacher can put students into pairs, it is not recommended except in very small classes because it can create too many groups. Similarly, while there can be five or more students per group, it is not recommended because it can be hard for that many students to successfully collaborate together in the amount of time given.

After the teacher has broken students up by groups, each group receives a notecard with one word or concept on it. The group then has 10–15 minutes to come up with a short skit that represents the word—without saying the word itself. All students in the performing group are expected to participate in the scene.

When the 10–15 minutes are up, the teacher has the students sit down with their groups. The teacher writes all the words/concepts up on the board. While the first group performs, the audience members try to determine which word or concept the performing group is portraying. At the end of the performance, the performing group announces ". . . and scene!" and that is the cue for the audience members to vote in their groups for which word or concept they think was portrayed. While the audience groups discuss their votes, the teacher conferences quietly with the performing group to provide feedback.

The key is that in addition to assessing the performing students on their scene, the teacher also calls on several students in the audience after each performance to explain why their groups voted the way that they did (majority rules for the group's vote, but an individual can explain why they did or did not agree with their group's vote).

Category of Cognitive Process Dimension

The task itself is at the Create level, and can evaluate standards from the Remember to Evaluate levels.

Learning Management

This is a wonderful activity to get students moving, engaged, and to help the teacher see what they really know; however, it does take some scaffolding to implement in the classroom. Once students know how to do this task it can quickly become their favorite and be a rich tool for the teacher to diagnose misconceptions other tasks might miss.

Because it is often difficult for students to learn both content and a new skill (such as this task) at the same time, the teacher might want to teach the task before marrying it with the content being taught. A teacher therefore might first want to start by putting students in groups (or even pairs if group work has not been done before) and giving them all the same, easy concept to act out, such as "the letter A." Most students will individually make the letter A the first time; then the teacher tells them they have to work together to create the letter A, rather than individual As.

After that, the teacher can give all students the same easy word or concept from the content, such as "rectangle" for mathematics. The teacher should have all students show their rectangles and then discuss different ways the groups chose to represent this, emphasizing there is no one "right" answer to portraying a concept, and having students note what worked well in other groups' portrayals.

The teacher will also want to work with students on how to provide constructive feedback to one another during the audience portion. For instance, rather than saying, "I didn't understand what they were doing at all," students should give comments such as, "At first I thought they were portraying cumulus clouds, but then they showed rainy weather, and I found that confusing."

It is also recommended the teacher allow students to access books and other materials while coming up with their scenes and as audience members. This helps to fill in any gaps in knowledge and can prevent them from simply standing there and saying, "I don't know."

Using the Data Effectively

The teacher should keep a list of all students on a checklist and assess them individually for content understanding during both the scene portrayal and the audience portion of the task.

Modifying and Differentiating the Strategy

There are many ways to modify this task! For younger students, it is best to keep it simple, but you can add any of the following modifications as students become more adept at the task to keep it fresh:

- No one can speak.
- Everyone must speak.
- Everyone must move at least once.
- Someone must be standing, someone must be sitting, and someone must be kneeling at all times.

Examples by Subject

English Language Arts

This works especially well to have students act out vocabulary words, but also important scenes in literature or concepts from informational texts.

Mathematics

Believe it or not, this task works great with mathematics! In addition to acting out vocabulary, students should be encouraged to act out real-world situations in which a computational method, property, or formula would be used. It can be especially beneficial for students who otherwise struggle with mathematics by having students use a different part of their brain to process mathematical ideas.

Science

In addition to acting out vocabulary words, students can perform skits showing how they would test various scientific principles or scientific developments in history.

Social Studies

Social studies is ripe for this task! Students can act out scenes from history, geographic locations or principles, psychological concepts or ideas, and much more.

World Languages

This is a great method for students to remember vocabulary. They can act out vocabulary words in the language and practice their speaking and fluency through a prepared scene.

Music

Students can act out vocabulary words, scenes from history, musical genres, and more.

Visual Arts

This is a great way to have students use a different part of their brains to act out artistic principles and methods, or to reenact famous works of art.

Health/Physical Education

Students can act out various exercises and the class can determine which muscle group the students are targeting. In health, students can act out various concepts such as nutrition, bodily systems, and healthy decisions.

Library/Media

The teacher can have students act out the various steps in the inquiry method, research methods and tools, or proper library procedures.

Career and Technical Education

Students in ROTC can reenact drills; students in economics can portray vocabulary terms; students in healthcare fields can create sketches of emergency response treatments to various situations.

The Task from Start to Finish

Identify

Serena Jacobs teaches fourth grade and is completing a unit on the Constitutional Convention with her students. She wants to provide them a chance to review before their assessment and clear up any last-minute misconceptions, so she decides to do the . . . And Scene! task with students. Her students have done this task multiple times before, so she is able to jump right in.

Plan

Serena uses her district's Social Studies curriculum and unpacks the following standard:

- Learners will understand the role of key leaders at the Constitutional Convention and compare/contrast their major contributions (George Washington, James Madison, George Mason, Roger Sherman).

- Learners will be able to describe the major branches of government.

Phrase	Cognitive Process Dimension Category	Reasoning
Learners will understand the role of key leaders at the Constitutional Convention and compare/contrast their major contributions (George Washington, James Madison, George Mason, Roger Sherman).	Understand	In this standard, students are using two of the cognitive processes under the Understand category. First, they have to be able to summarize the roles of the named historical figures, and second they have to be able to compare them.
Learners will be able to describe the major branches of government.	Understand	In this standard, learners are showing their understanding of the major branches of government by putting the information in their own words.

Serena knows the . . . And Scene! task will work well with this standard because students will have to compare/contrast what they know about several of the key individuals at the Constitutional Convention in order to create their scenes and identify which scenes others are portraying.

Apply

Serena has 27 students and she breaks up into seven groups (six groups of four and one group of three). She has each of the terms written on a different note card and has one person from each group randomly choose a note card. She then allows students 15 minutes to put together their scenes while she checks in with each group to make sure they have an idea and to provide feedback while they plan. She reminds each group to practice their scene at least twice and provides reminders at the 10-, 5-, and 2-minute marks.

Afterward, she has all students sit with their groups and gives each group a marker board and a marker. She projects all nine terms on the whiteboard. Groups go one at a time to deliver their scenes, after which Serena tells the audience members to guess what term the group was portraying while she delivers feedback to the group on their scene. Serena makes sure to call on each student at least once during their time as audience member.

When the last group performs, there are still three vocabulary words left, so the audience cannot simply use the process of elimination.

Assess

During the performances, Serena fills out the following chart:

2 = strongly demonstrates understanding; 1 = moderately demonstrates understanding; 0 = demonstrates little or no understanding

Word/ Concept	Students	Scene Score	Audience Score	Notes
Thomas Jefferson	Mariah	1	2	Founding Fathers riding in car to CC?
	Tordyah	1	2	Founding Fathers riding in car to CC?
	Taevon	1	2	Founding Fathers riding in car to CC?
	Livia	1	2	Founding Fathers riding in car to CC?

Bill of Rights	Pablo	2	2	
	Rose	2	1	Vague answer when called on for "legislative"
	Cecilia	2	2	
	Robert	2	2	
Legislative	Nora	2	2	
	Bruno	2	1	Vague answer when called on for R.S.
	Cole	2	2	
	Tremaine	2	2	
Judicial	Riley	2	2	
	Daniel	2	2	
	Katie	2	2	
	Sasha	2	2	
Roger Sherman	Rupert	2	2	
	August	2	1	Could not answer first time called on for A. of C.; answered second time for J.M.
	Ivy	2	2	
	Sean	2	2	
George Mason	Sincere	2	2	
	Bella	2	2	
	Tomas	2	2	
	Richard	2	2	
James Madison	Matilda	2	0	Called on twice; could not answer either time.
	Jude	2	2	
	Ben	2	2	

As you can see from her chart, most students did very well on this activity. Serena was surprised to see one group act out the Founding Fathers riding together in a car; this is a misconception one would have never thought to address with fourth graders and a more traditional assessment of learning might not have caught. She does a quick activity with the whole class afterwards to demonstrate the time period of the Constitutional Convention and remind them of what life was like during that time.

She also pulls all the students who gave vague answers into a small group to play another review game before the assessment; she follows up one-on-one with Matilda during lunch and goes over several of the concepts with her.

Refine

As they have in the past, Serena's students enjoy the . . . And Scene! activity, and she knows she will do it again for another unit. She decides to make it more challenging next time she will introduce the "Standing, Sitting, Kneeling" rule to see how her students do with it.

Check In, Check Out

  Description

This task combines movement with collaborative work and is a great way to formatively assess during a learning activity.

Before the lesson, the teacher will lay out numbered task cards in a central area of the classroom. Teachers can have fun with the layout of the task cards; we have seen teachers arrange the cards in a "bay" while discussing marine life, or in a formation like a boat for a unit on the Civil War, or even just in a hopscotch pattern. For this particular example, we will use a 4 × 4 grid like this:

1	2	3	4
5	6	7	8
9	10	11	12
13	14	15	16

On each task card the front is the number of the task and on the back is an activity on the current topic students must complete.

An example of a task could be, "Write three (3) antonyms for 'big'" or "Order the following events in the Civil War from first to last" or "Identify the independent variable in the write-up of an experiment below." Whatever the task, students should be able to write a quick, short answer.

Therefore, a task card might look like this:

[Front]	[Back]
7	Write three sentences that express an opinion.

Students work together in pairs. They go "fishing" by choosing a task card (explain that it does not matter the order they complete them), reading the task card together, and then completing the task together.

Each student should have a sheet that mirrors the layout of the task cards. The students write the answer in the appropriate box on their sheets.

Before students can return one task card to get another, they take their work to the teacher, who quickly reviews it and provides immediate feedback. If the answer is correct, the teacher put a check in that box. If it is incorrect, the teacher puts a tally in the box, gives students feedback, and has them go back and work on the answer some more, then bring it back. If the second time the pair returns they get it right, the teacher adds a check; if the answer is still wrong, the teacher puts another tally. Depending on how close students are to the correct answer, the teacher can choose whether to have them keep working on this task or choose another one.

Category of Cognitive Process Dimension

This task works best for the Remember through Analyze levels. It can also be used for Evaluate or Create, but due to limited spaces in the boxes for answering, it is not ideal for those levels, which often require more time, thought, and space.

Learning Management

The teacher tells students beforehand how many checks they must get in order to complete the activity. It is recommended that teachers require fewer checks than there are task cards so no pairs are left waiting on one or two task cards at the end.

It is also recommended that teachers assign each pair their starting number, so students are not rushing to retrieve the same task first. The teacher will also want to show students how to properly return the task cards and materials.

For tasks that require more materials than just the task card, it is recommended the teacher use plastic bags to house all the materials. For instance, the teacher might include a short passage or book for students to read and answer comprehension questions, or a ruler to measure the length of an object, or dice to roll and multiply the numbers together.

It is also recommended the teacher have an answer sheet at the ready to quickly check answers and move students on their way. The teacher should also stand in an area where students can form an orderly line to await feedback, and might need to model for students how to stand appropriately assuming there is a line.

While students can work in groups of three or more, pairs is really the preferred option to ensure everyone has a chance to participate in the work.

Using the Data Effectively

In addition to providing students with immediate feedback, teachers can use the data to see how much support students required in order to address the task cards.

Modifying and Differentiating the Strategy

Teachers can arrange the task cards in specific orders from lower to higher level. In our example above, for instance, 1–4 might be tasks at the Remember level, 5–8 might be at the Understand level, 9–12 at the Apply level, and 13–16 at the Analyze level. A teacher might require students to complete one task card from each row, or assign some groups to complete 1–8 while others complete tasks 9–16.

For pre-readers, the teacher can do a similar activity, but with fewer tasks and relying on pictures instead of works. For instance, the teacher might just have the number "3" on the task card, and students have to draw three of something. Or the teacher might have the letter "B" on the task card, and students have to say a word that starts with the letter "B" in order to earn their check mark.

Examples by Subject

English Language Arts

This works especially well with short passages and comprehension questions, but can also be used with topics such as synonym/antonyms, vocabulary development, fact/opinion, character analysis, and more.

Mathematics

Short word problems are especially effective with this activity. It is also a great way to incorporate real-world applications into the classroom ("Find the area of your desk," or "Find the volume of the tissue box in centimeters").

Science

Students can be given examples of experiments and asked to find the independent and dependent variable, or determine what variables will need to be controlled, or give examples of how an example experiment could be made more rigorous. Students can also be asked to draw a quick graph based on a table of data, or evaluate a claim based on provided data.

Social Studies

Tasks might include sequencing events, reading an excerpt from a primary source and answering questions, comparing/contrasting people or events, or drawing and labeling a diagram.

World Languages

Students might read short passages in the language being studied and answer comprehension questions, write down three phrases they might need to know if completing a certain task (such as ordering food in a restaurant), or compare and contrast their culture with the culture being studied.

Music

The task card might have examples of time signatures, volume or tempo designations, or forms such as cadenza or coda, and be asked to find examples of each in music they are performing.

Visual Arts

Task cards might have an example of a work of art along with questions at various levels for students to answer (e.g., "What time period does this artwork belong to?" "What artist created this work?" "What major art elements do you see in this artwork?"), or students might compare/contrast two works of art, or read a short biography about an artist and answer questions.

Health/Physical Education

Students can answer questions about ways to increase core strength, or review nutrition labels and evaluate the healthiness of the particular food, or read scenarios about students confronted with risky situations and write one or two sentences about what students should do next.

Library/Media

Students can write the call numbers for various books, determine how many books the library has on a certain subject, or find a book to read a short passage from it and answer questions.

Career and Technical Education

Students can answer sample questions from certification exams.

The Task from Start to Finish

Identify

LaTanya Jefferson teaches high school mathematics and is finishing up her four-week Introduction to Statistics unit. Before giving the summative assessment, LaTanya wants to see what her students know and what they still need to work on, so two days before the assessment, she decides to do the Check In, Check Out task. Based on the results, she can determine whole group lessons and what she needs to work on with individuals.

Plan

LaTanya has 18 students in her class. She decides to have them work in nine pairs. For the activity, she lays out task cards in the following formation.

1	2	3
4	5	6
7	8	9
10	11	12

The tasks represent the four Common Core Mathematics standards students worked with during this unit as follows:

Row A Tasks 1–3	IC.B.3 Recognize the purposes of and differences among sample surveys, experiments, and observational studies; explain how randomization relates to each.
Row B Tasks 4–6	IC.B.4 Use data from a sample survey to estimate a population mean or proportion; develop a margin of error through the use of simulation models for random sampling.
Row C Tasks 7–9	IC.B.5 Use data from a randomized experiment to compare two treatments; use simulations to decide if differences between parameters are significant.
Row D Tasks 10–12	IC.B.6 Evaluate reports based on data. Write a function that describes a relationship between two quantities.

LaTanya unpacks the standards as follows.

Phrase	Cognitive Process Dimension Category	Reasoning
IC.B.3 Recognize the purposes of and differences among sample surveys, experiments, and observational studies; explain how randomization relates to each.	Understand	Students are using the Comparing cognitive process in the Understand category of Bloom's Revised Taxonomy in order to recognize the purposes and different among surveys, experiments, and observational studies; they must also be able to put into their own words how randomization relates to each.

IC.B.4 Use data from a sample survey to estimate a population mean or proportion; develop a margin of error through the use of simulation models for random sampling.	Apply	Students are using data from a sample survey to estimate a population mean or proportion and develop a margin of error with simulation models; they are applying a process to a new situation in order to find an answer.
IC.B.5 Use data from a randomized experiment to compare two treatments; use simulations to decide if differences between parameters are significant.	Apply	Students are applying procedures for how to determine whether a difference is significant to data in a randomized experiment.
IC.B.6 Evaluate reports based on data. Write a function that describes a relationship between two quantities.	Evaluate	Students should be using a set of criteria in order to evaluate whether the data supports claims in the reports.

Apply

LaTanya puts students in pairs and tells them they need to complete at least one task card per row. For each row, the task cards are similar enough so that no matter which card students choose, their answers will yield similar data about their abilities.

Example of Task Card 1:

Researchers want to study the relationship between how well third-grade students do on a test of multiplication facts at the end of the year and how well they do on their end-of-year

Algebra II standardized assessments. They randomly choose 100 Algebra II students in the nearest school district and look at their end of third grade multiplication facts assessments and their end-of-year Algebra II standardized assessment scores and determine that there is a relationship.

1. What type of research design is this: a survey, observational study, or experiment? How do you know?

2. Why would the researchers choose this type of design rather than either of the other two listed above?

3. How could the researchers have increased randomization of their sample and how would that strengthen the validity of the research?

Task Cards 2 and 3 feature different research examples, but have the same questions.

Assess

LaTanya assigns two students to work together: Ben and Kaia. When Ben and Kaia complete Task Card 1 and bring their work to LaTanya, they have the following answers for this task card:

1. Observational study because they did not purposefully apply a treatment, they just looked at what students already did. They didn't survey anyone.

2. The study would take too many years to be an experiment. People could lie about their scores on their surveys.

3. Use more than one school district because what if they picked a school district where all the parents hire tutors for their kids or something like that.

She decides that the answer Ben and Kaia provide for #1, while not particularly detailed, shows they have a good working definition of the different types of studies. For #2, she tells them some experiments do take years, and to brainstorm another reason why this could not be an experiment and gives them the hint to think about what it means for a study to be an experiment. She also asks them to give one more way the researchers could have increased validity for #3. She writes one tally mark in the top corner of their answer box.

Ben and Kaia return to their desks, work for a few more minutes, and bring her back these updated answers:

2. You can't assign some kids to fail and others to pass their tests in order to apply a treatment because it's unethical.

3. They could use more than 100 students.

LaTanya decides these are better answers and gives them a check mark.

After the lesson, LaTanya collects all student papers and reviews them, coming up with the following chart:

Task #	Standard	Needed to Fix Answer Once/ Minimal Review Needed	Needed to Fix Answer More Than Once/Significant Review Needed
Row A Tasks 1–3	IC.B.3 Recognize the purposes of and differences among sample surveys, experiments, and observational studies; explain how randomization relates to each.	Kaia, Ben Jackie, Jorge Luis, Sam	Raina, Max
Row B Tasks 4–6	IC.B.4 Use data from a sample survey to estimate a population mean or proportion; develop a margin of error through the use of simulation models for random sampling.	Charlotte, Ruby Ezra, Drake Jackie, Jorge Kaia, Ben	Raina, Max Luis, Sam
Row C Tasks 7–9	IC.B.5 Use data from a randomized experiment to compare two treatments; use simulations to decide if differences between parameters are significant.	Luis, Sam Ezra, Drake Destiny, Lyle Shilek, Ethan	Raina, Max Jackie, Jorge
Row D Tasks 10–12	IC.B.6 Evaluate reports based on data. Write a function that describes a relationship between two quantities.	Luis, Sam Amelia, Lyla Jackie, Jorge	Raina, Max

The next two days before the test, LaTanya knows that she will have to work significantly with Raina and Max, and probably also quite a bit with Luis, Sam, Jackie, and Jorge. She asks these students to come during their lunch periods to work with her and also assigns them some extra practice sets before the assessment.

During the these two days, LaTanya also has the students work on some open-ended practical application problems, and uses the collaborative work time to pull students who require review for each standard for mini-lessons in small groups.

Refine

In order to differentiate, LaTanya allowed groups who finished early to complete more task cards. She decides that next time she will also keep a list of those students who completed more than the required number of task cards so that during the two-day assessment review period, she can provide them with more challenging work.

Group Graphic Organizers

■ Description

Graphic organizers are great for helping students activate prior learning, plan upcoming projects or writing, or organize information they have learned. It can also be helpful to have students work in groups on graphic organizers for collaborative projects, but this runs into a problem central to all collaborative work: how will you know who has contributed what?

In this task, students work together to create poster-size graphic organizers—the key is that each student uses a different color marker. This, therefore, gives them the benefits of working together while allowing the teacher to quickly assess who contributed what.

One of the keys to this is to first model for students how to work together, especially when it comes to the balance between speaking up when they have an idea and ensuring their group members also get a chance to speak.

■ Category of Cognitive Process Dimension

Depending on the type of graphic organizer used, this strategy can incorporate every level of Bloom's Revised Taxonomy. Students might use graphic organizers to simply record information to recall later (Remember); students might put information into their own words (Understand); if students use a graphic organizer to work through a process (such as an experiment or solving a Mathematics problem), they would be working at the application level. Graphic organizers in which students compare/contrast in order to show how elements support themes have students work at the Analyze level, while graphic organizers that help students to consider information and evidence in order to make and justify a decisions represent the Evaluate level. Lastly, graphic organizers that help students plan a new project, story, invention, or a similar product would all facilitate work at the Create level.

 ## Learning Management

It will probably be necessary to model to students how to work together collaboratively so everyone's ideas are shared. If students are not used to collaborative work, you can use smaller groups and make a rule that one person shares and writes something, then another person, and so on. It might also be necessary to give students some "starter" ideas as a whole group.

 ## Using the Data Effectively

Teachers can use the data from the collaborative graphic organizer to determine which groups need more support and in which ways when having students work together in groups. If groups are working together for multiple lessons, the teacher should quickly review any collaborative graphic organizer after each lesson (as well as monitoring during the lesson). Teachers can tell the extent to which students are participating to work with groups and individuals both on their content knowledge and skills as well as their collaborative abilities.

Modifying and Differentiating the Strategy

Teachers with students who are not strong writers should not be afraid to use graphic organizers! For example, a preschool teacher can use hula hoops to create Venn Diagrams and give students objects or pictures to sort. For collaborative graphic organizers, teachers can give each student a different set of colored cards and ask them when they sort an object to first put down a colored card and then the object. This way the teacher will be able to see who has sorted which object where.

For older students who are at lower readiness levels, the teacher can make the rule that everyone has to share and write (or even draw) one or two ideas, but can do more if they wish, therefore allowing students to contribute different amounts of information.

Examples by Subject

English Language Arts

This works especially well for pre-writing, but can also be used for vocabulary development and plotting story elements, among other topics.

Mathematics

Graphic organizers can be used in the Mathematics classroom to help students attack real-life scenarios or word problems, and they can also be used to compare/contrast formulas, shapes, and other concepts.

Science

In Science, students might use graphic organizers to compare/contrast concepts, to plan and execute experiments, and to develop questions for case studies.

Social Studies

Students can use graphic organizers to compare/contrast events or the lives of famous historical figures, to sequence events, or to show facts surrounding concepts.

World Languages

Graphic organizers can be used to brainstorm vocabulary words that might be associated with specific tasks or events, to show knowledge of another culture, or to sequence events in another culture's history.

Music

Comparing and contrasting musical pieces, sequencing musical pieces or genres in history, and organizing information about playing and singing techniques are all ways in which students can use graphic organizers in music.

Visual Arts

Similar to music, students might compare/contrast works of art or artists, sequence works of art or artists in history, organize techniques, or plan their ideas for upcoming projects.

Health/Physical Education

In Health, students can complete cause/effect graphic organizers about various choices and their impacts on potential health; in P.E., students can use graphic organizers to create and document progress on health plans.

Library/Media

Students can use graphic organizers to outline questions for research topics, determine what sources they will look at to find information, and record their research and evaluate the sources.

Career and Technical Education

Graphic organizers are a great way for students to organize information regarding certifications in order to study for assessments.

The Task from Start to Finish

Identify

Jerry Ross teaches fifth-grade writing. Previous data on both standardized assessments and district-level benchmarks indicate that students traditionally struggle both with essay organization and with persuasive essays.

Plan

Jerry uses these Common Core Reading: Foundational Skills standards:

CCSS.ELA-LITERACY.W.5.1.   Write opinion pieces on topics or texts, supporting a point of view with reasons and information.

CCSS.ELA-LITERACY.W.5.1.A.   Introduce a topic or text clearly, state an opinion, and create an organizational structure in which ideas are logically grouped to support the writer's purpose.

Phrase	Cognitive Process Dimension Category	Reasoning
CCSS.ELA-LITERACY.W.5.1 Write opinion pieces on topics or texts, supporting a point of view with reasons and information. CCSS.ELA-LITERACY.W.5.1.A Introduce a topic or text clearly, state an opinion, and create an organizational structure in which ideas are logically grouped to support the writer's purpose.	Evaluate and Create	The main thrust of this standard is to have students evaluate; that is, they are choosing a viewpoint and then supporting it with evidence. The project students are using to show their evaluation, however, is a written piece, which is at the Create level.

Apply

Jerry decides to have his students work in pairs to choose a point of view on this topic: Should students wear be required to wear uniforms to school?

Before they begin to write, Jerry splits his 27 students into nine groups of three. Each group has a T chart on a poster-sized piece of paper; one column says "Reasons FOR" and the other says "Reasons AGAINST." He explains to students they should come up with a list of at least three reasons for and three reasons against—later, they will do a gallery walk of all the posters in order to help them determine whether they want to write a paper FOR uniforms or AGAINST, and choose their supporting evidence.

Jerry gives each group three markers: blue, red, and green. He has each student sign his or her name at the bottom of the poster in his or her assigned color so he can easily tell who contributed what. He explains that each student must contribute at least two times, though it can be to either side of the chart (as long as the whole group has at least three reasons for both columns). Students are allowed to contribute more if they desire.

Lastly, he reminds students their role for this activity is not to critique each other, but rather to encourage and build on one another's ideas. Therefore, there are no "wrong" contributions to the chart, as long as they relate to the topic. Although he has done this activity with students before, he takes one minute to model an inappropriate negative comment on another student's contribution, asks students what he did wrong, and then has a student model a more appropriate response.

Assess

For the purposes of this book, student names will be included in the example below. In real life, of course, the work would be color-coded and students would not have to write their names after each contribution.

Overall, as Jerry walks around to monitor students, he notices groups quickly fill up the "Reasons AGAINST" column, but many struggle to come up with three reasons for the "Reasons FOR" column. He works with two groups one-on-one before realizing multiple groups are struggling, at which point he stops class to do a quick "whole group" brainstorm before having students return to their group work.

While he quickly monitors student contributions during class, Jerry takes an even closer look at the students' work afterward. This is an example from one of the groups:

Reasons FOR School Uniforms	Reasons AGAINST School Uniforms
Less time to pick out what to wear in the morning (Amaya)	I like to express my creativity through my clothes (Amaya)
Faster (Juniper)	My right to choose my clothes (Saul)
Cheaper (Saul)	Kids should wear whatever they want (Juniper)
Harder to be made fun of (Amaya)	Makes parents buy more clothes for kids (Saul)
Not everyone can afford "cool" clothes (Amaya)	Uniforms are unflattering (Amaya)

Jerry notices several things from this chart. Amaya seems to have ideas on both sides of the debate that reflect higher-level thinking. Jerry notes when students start working on their individual graphic organizers for their actual essays, he will probably only need to check in quickly with Amaya.

He also notices in addition to contributing the minimum, Juniper's contribution under Reasons FOR is really just reiterating Amaya's previous idea, and her idea under Reasons AGAINST is very general. Jerry notes that he will need to check in frequently with Juniper during the individual portion of the writing assignment. Knowing Juniper's previous reluctance to write, he also decides that he will scaffold the individual portion for her by pulling her and three other students who struggled during the collaborative brainstorm into a small group to plan together.

Lastly, Jerry notices that Saul contributed three (rather than two) ideas and that his ideas, though not as well-defined as Amaya's, are specific and on-topic. He notes to check in a couple of times with Saul during the independent graphic organizer portion of the pre-writing.

After quickly reviewing all nine graphic organizers, Jerry is able to make this table to help him differentiate the next day's lesson:

Check in Once	Check in 2–3 Times	Pull for Small Group at Start of Lesson
Amaya	Arya	Juniper
Lance	Thomas	Henry
Galli	Brighton	Terrence
Jamal	Elizabeth	Melanie
William	Berkley	
Donte	Jordan	
Kendra	Jonas	
Maria	Raekwon	
Adah	Makai	
	Shellis	
	Saul	
	Rhianna	
	Susannah	
	Eshan	

Refine

Jerry decides that next time, in addition to formatively assessing students based on their work, he will also have them self-assess by rating how ready they think they are to work independently, so that a 3 = I'm ready to go; 2 = Think I'll be good but check on me; and 3 = I'm confused and would like more help. He thinks that will help him further refine his formative assessment in terms of helping students with their independent work.

Learning Upgrade Charts

 Description

This strategy can be considered an upgrade to the ever-popular K-W-L chart. One of the biggest problems with the K-W-L chart comes with the K—"What do I Know?" in which students write down information they already know about a given topic. The problem is that often students have vaguely remembered details or outright misconceptions. Similarly, without an introduction to the learning, it can be hard for them to think answer the prompt "What Do I Want to Know?" Lastly, a single column for "What I Learned" (which takes place after the learning) does not help students to organize their new learning.

Instead, try using a chart like this with students:

What We Think We Know	Were We Right?	. . . Or Not Quite?	Corrected and/or Added Information:
New Learning:			

The first column is completed by students before the learning takes place. The next two columns are completed as students explore the topic, marking each of their "Think We Knows" as either "right" or "not quite."

It works best to have students work in pairs or small groups to complete the charts. As the students move through the learning (either throughout the unit or the lesson), they check in with one another to revisit their chart and mark their "think we knows" in either the "right" or "not quite" column. If they were incorrect, they write the corrected statement in the "Corrected and/or Added Information" column. Even if they were correct, they can add information on the particular topic to this column to show their new learning.

Students should also work on filling in the "New Learning" section of the graphic organizer during the lesson or unit.

Category of Cognitive Process Dimension

The chart can work with the Remember through Create categories because it can be used to sum up any learning that takes place in the classroom.

Learning Management

It will be necessary to show students how to fill out the chart at each stage the first time a teacher uses this task with students. It is recommended the teacher choose a topic, model for the students how to brainstorm what to write in the "What I Think I Know" column, then read a short passage on the particular topic, meanwhile marking the "right" or "not quite" columns, correcting information, and lastly, adding the new learning.

Depending on the particular topic, students may also need some whole-group prompting to "jog their memories" regarding previously learned information. It may be helpful to post a "key word" bank (without defining the words) to help activate prior knowledge.

This task works best in pairs and therefore the teacher will want to pay careful attention to how students are grouped and may need to provide lessons beforehand on how to work together productively. While students can work together to brainstorm ideas, we recommend that if possible, both students complete a graphic organizer for themselves so they have it to refer back to later or use to study.

We recommended also the teacher have the students complete the "What I Think I Know" part of the graphic organizer at least a day ahead of time so the teacher can review the answers and design instruction around student learning needs.

Using the Data Effectively

The teacher will want to review the graphic organizer at the beginning of the unit to determine what students do and do not know, and what misconceptions there are, in order to plan either the lesson or unit. Teachers should also check in with students periodically throughout the learning to ensure that they are updating their charts and to make sure any misconceptions have been corrected and new learning is being added.

Modifying and Differentiating the Strategy

It may be better to complete the graphic organizer as a whole group (copies can be distributed to the class if desired) for younger students who are not strong writers. Older students who have difficulty writing can work with a partner who is a stronger writer and then have a copy made.

Examples by Subject

These examples are questions that could be used for the various subject areas.

English Language Arts

What do you think you know about Shakespeare's *Hamlet*?

Mathematics

What do you think you know about finding area?

Science

What do you think you know about gravitation?

Social Studies

What do you think you know about the Medieval Age?

World Languages

What do you think you know about Julius Caesar?

Music

What do you think you know about sonatas?

Visual Arts

What do you think you know about the history of 3D animation?

Health/Physical Education

What do you think you know about proper hydration during physical activity?

Library/Media

What do you think you know about procedures for using copyrighted material?

Career and Technical Education

What do you think you know about applying for a small business loan?

The Task from Start to Finish

Identify

Yoshi Aki teaches sixth grade Physical Education. She is teaching a unit entitled Energy In/Energy Out on the balance of energy. It is a six-lesson unit and she wants to know what her students already know about the concepts.

Plan

Yoshi refers to her district's standards for this unit:

The student will be able to describe the balance between energy expenditure and energy input, including the roles played by nutrition and physical activity in maintaining the balance.

Phrase	Cognitive Process Dimension Category	Reasoning
The student will be able to describe the balance between energy expenditure and energy input, including the roles played by nutrition and physical activity in maintaining the balance.	Understand	In order to meet this standard, students are using the Explaining cognitive process to construct meaning about the balance of energy expenditure and energy input.

Yoshi decides to use the Learning Upgrade Chart to see what students already know and help them organize their learning throughout the unit.

Apply

On the last day of the previous unit Yoshi puts her students into pairs and introduces the topic for their next unit: Energy In/Energy Out. She tells her students she is interested in finding out what they already know so she can tailor the learning activities to them. She puts the following key words on the board: nutrition, meal planning, body composition, moderate/vigorous exercise, food groups, hydration, and macronutrients.

Yoshi then gives students 10 minutes to work together to each fill out the "What I Think I Know" column on their Learning Upgrade Chart. At the end of each lesson during the unit, Yoshi gives students 10 minutes to work with their partner again to mark the "right" or "not quite" column, correct or add information, and fill in the "New Learning" section.

Assess

Yoshi reviews her students' Learning Upgrade Charts after each lesson to see how students are progressing. Here is an example of a completed chart (for Darius, working with Yasmine) and how Yoshi used it during the course of the unit:

What We Think We Know	Were We Right?	. . . Or Not Quite?	Corrected and/or Added Information:
You need exercise to work off calories.	X		You also need calories so that you can exercise.
Vigorous exercise is better.		X	Half-right. Vigorous exercise seems to better for your heart but some exercise is better than none. So even if you only have moderate exercise that's better than nothing. And different types of exercises have different benefits.
Macronutrients are the best kind of food for you.	X		Macronutrients are the types of foods we eat, like fat, protein, carbohydrates. You need some of all of them but in the right amounts.
You have to drink a lot of water to stay healthy.	X		Most people need to multiply their body weight times two-thirds to figure out how much water they need and add 12 ounces of water for every 30 minutes you work out.

You have to eat from each food group every day to stay healthy.	X		But you need to eat more of some and less of others.

New Learning:
Kids should exercise 60 or more minutes a day total (doesn't all have to be at the same time). Should include aerobic exercise and strengthening exercises. How much you should eat depends on how tall you are, how active you are, and other stuff.
Whole fruits are better than juice.
I can set SMART goals to help myself be more active and healthy. I need to improve my flexibility and endurance.

When Yoshi first reviewed Darius's and Yasmine's work and their "What I Think I Know" column, she saw they already knew many of the basics of the units (the importance of exercise, hydration, and eating well). She does notice they, and many of their peers, tend to think in generalities ("Vigorous exercise is better," "You have to drink a lot of water") and she decides to use some of these generalities as a starting statement for her daily lessons and then help students to understand the statements more fully.

She also notices one misconception in particular: "Macronutrients are the best kind of food for you." She reviews other charts, and notices most students either do not mention macronutrients at all or else have misconceptions about what macronutrients are. Yoshi makes notes to emphasize this term and allots more time to the topic than she originally planned.

As she reviews the "Corrected and/or Added Information" column and the "New Learning" section, Yoshi is able to tell when her students fully grasp a topic and when she needs to review it the next day. For instance, the only thing Darius writes about the lesson on food groups is "Whole fruits are better than juice." Yoshi notices other students also include similar details rather than main ideas, so she revisits the lesson the next day and specifically does a whole group mini-lesson on the main ideas from the day before.

Refine

Next time, Yoshi decides that in addition to pairing up students, that at least twice during the unit she will have the pairs work with another pair to further check their learning with one another, making sure to strategically connect pairs who appear to understand the concept with ones who seem to struggle to write down the main ideas.

Professional Development Plan
Collaborative Tasks

Step 1

Read the chapter in advance of meeting as a group. Ask teachers to reflect on their own experiences with collaborative learning activities before coming to the meeting. Consider the times when cooperative grouping activities worked well and times where the plan did not go as intended. Ask them to bring successful cooperative activity lessons learned (positive examples) to the professional development meeting.

Step 2

In a face-to-face professional development session that is approximately one hour in length:

- Place teachers in heterogeneous groupings with three to four teachers in each group.

- Ask teachers to discuss successful and not successful cooperative grouping experiences in about 10 minutes. This is a brief discussion and they will have more time in the next part of the activity.

- After everyone has shared in the group, explain they will create a T chart. One column will list characteristics of effective collaborative tasks and the other column will list characteristics of ineffective tasks. Ask for a brief explanation for each characteristic and have the teachers use different colors within each of their groups (i.e., one has a blue marker, one has a red marker, etc.). Ask the group to take 20 minutes.

- After 20 minutes, ask all participants to take a 10 minute gallery walk.

- Upon conclusion of the gallery walk, prompt dialogue within the group about what the teachers saw. How can they use lessons learned from their colleagues in the upcoming two weeks when they are engaged in active use of Collaborative formative assessment strategies?

- Give participants this task: "Use at least one of the Collaborative formative assessment techniques in your class over the next week and be ready to discuss how it went." Optional: require participants to try out two of the tasks.

Step 3

Conduct walkthroughs as staff implement the Collaborative formative assessment strategies over the next week. Consider collaborative walkthroughs as well as individual peer walkthroughs.

Step 4

In a follow-up face-to-face professional development session:

- Ask the same groups from the previous session to develop an . . . And Scene! simulated lesson that demonstrates one or more successes with their Collaborative strategy implementation. Allow the groups 20 minutes to develop a three-to-four minute skit (cap the skit at four minutes and keep close track of time).

- Depending on the number of groups, either have all groups perform their skits or divide up the groups so everyone sees at least four skits.

- Put participants in groups (either heterogeneous or with like grade levels/subject areas). Have each group discuss the following reflection questions:

  - What task did you try? What worked well? What might you do differently next time?

- What instructional decisions did you make based on the task?

- How will you use this professional development to make a change in your practice that positively impacts your students and their achievement?

PART III

Movement: Formative Assessment Strategies
Integrating Movement into Formative Assessments

Think back to a professional development session you have attended that you found particularly boring. What did that professional development look like and feel like? Did you spend the majority of the time sitting? Chances are good that you did, and if so, it probably contributed more to your struggle to pay attention. While you may remember being bored at the professional development, do you remember what you learned? Again, chances are good that you did not.

The same difficulty to "sit and get" often occurs in our students (and especially if they already find the content abstract or not relevant). Thankfully, there are some quick and easy tasks you can incorporate into your classroom to get your students up, moving, and learning.

The Body–Mind Connection

The major part of the brain involved in movement is the cerebellum, and even though the cerebellum itself only takes up about 10 percent of the total mass of the brain, it houses almost half of all the brain's neurons; moreover, the cerebellum has neural pathways from it that lead to the areas of the brain associated with memory, attention, and spatial perception (Jensen, 2005). Therefore, scientists theorize there exists a significant correlation between movement and learning.

Movement can impact our brains and their ability to learn in other ways, too. When students are active and moving, there are chemical alterations at the synapses that allow new content to be encoded for easier access and recall down the road (Armstrong, 2008). Even the simple act of standing during class can improve brain function by increasing blood, and therefore oxygen, flow to the brain by as much as 5 to 8 percent (Jensen, 2005). Just think about how refreshed you feel when you stand up and walk around, and the impact that walk has on your own personal productivity. The same holds true for your students. Passive students do not learn at the same rates or levels than those students that are active, moving, and engaged.

It is also important to note that the cerebellum continues to develop through adolescence and is particularly susceptible to environmental influences (Armstrong, 2016). Unfortunately, educators often believe that movement is more for younger students, preferring a more traditional lecture style for older students. The benefits that come from movement and exercise, though, are crucial for learners of all ages.

How Movement Impacts Learning

It should come as no surprise that several studies have shown that increased movement in the classroom leads to increased student achievement. Movement can help to build vocabulary by helping students create a mental image, and it is especially helpful for more abstract concepts (Lyding et al., 2014). Children can solve mathematical problems more quickly and accurately when they incorporate gestures rather than sitting on their hands (Goldin-Meadow et al., 1999, 2001). Similarly, studies have shown when students act out mathematical or scientific concepts, such as demonstrating different types of angles or how stars and planets move through space, they experienced increased academic success compared to more "traditional" sit-and-get methods (Shoval, 2011; Plummer, 2009).

Many people worry, however, that allowing students to move more in classrooms might lead to more off-task behaviors. However, many studies have begun to show the opposite: students who stand in class more tend to have higher participation in classroom discussions and fewer off-task behaviors (Davis, 2015).

Tips for Using Movement Tasks for Formative Assessment

- Students who are not used to moving in the classroom may be reluctant to do so the first few times you try some of these methods. Don't be deterred! In these cases, try especially hard to help them understand how the task is useful and relevant to their learning.

- The first time you try one of these tasks—and especially if students are not used to moving—keep in mind you may need to break up longer tasks into shorter segments. Model the task beforehand, including how to move around the classroom safely and while staying on-task.

- Ensure that your room arrangement allows students to move quickly and safely in order to decrease off-task behaviors.

Four Corners

Description

Four Corners is an "oldie but goodie" for formative assessment. The teacher gives students a prompt, posts potential answers in separate corners of the room, and then asks students to move to the corner that best represents the answer.

An important caveat here is that teachers who use prompts with concrete answers often report that rather than determining the answers on their own, students who are unsure of the answer usually "follow the crowd." This can make it hard for the teacher to know what the students really understand. Therefore, this task actually works best with prompts that do not have right-and-wrong answers, but require some critical thinking on the part of the students.

For instance, if the teacher labels the corners A, B, C, and D, and then asks the following question, students are likely to follow the crowd if they don't actually know the answer:

- Which Founding Father is known as the Father of Our Country?
    - George Washington
    - Thomas Jefferson
    - Alexander Hamilton
    - James Madison

It would be better, instead, to ask the following question:

- If time travel were possible, which Founding Father would you want to go back in time to visit?
  - George Washington
  - Thomas Jefferson
  - Alexander Hamilton
  - James Madison

Then, when students choose their corners, have them work with a partner to explain their reasoning. The teacher can also have students work together to create a one-minute persuasive presentation to convince others to join their corners.

For students with stronger writing abilities, the teacher should have students write a sentence to a paragraph about what they chose and why.

Category of Cognitive Process Dimension

The activity itself is at the Evaluate level, because it is asking students to make a choice and support their choice with evidence, and can be used with any standards up to that level.

It could also be used with standards up to the Create level by having students reflect on their own learning, such as the following example reflection for a narrative essay.

> How confident do you feel that your essay conveys your intended tone to your audience based on word choice, sentence structure, and organization? Be ready to explain why.

- Extremely Confident
- Confident
- Somewhat confident
- Not confident

Learning Management

The teacher will need to show students how to move around the room safely. It may be helpful to call groups of students to get up and move around the classroom on the teacher's cue, rather than having all students jump up at once. For instance, the teacher might say, "All students at Table 1, move to your chosen corner," or "All students who choose A, move there now."

 ## Using the Data Effectively

It is important that in addition to noting where students choose to stand around the room, the teacher also listens to students as they provide their explanations, or for older students, read their explanations and summaries of their discussions in their corners. The teacher should use this information to reteach and remediate with either individuals or the whole class as necessary.

 ## Modifying and Differentiating the Strategy

Younger students or English Language Learners may need simpler prompts and possibly pictures to help them remember which corner represents which choice. It might also be helpful to reduce the number of choices to two or three for these students.

Examples by Subject

English Language Arts

This example is a question that could be used in English Language Arts:

> Based on elements such as setting, character, and plot—which short story do you think is the quintessential example of gothic literature?

- Nathaniel Hawthorne's "The Wedding Knell"
- Edgar Allen Poe's "The Oval Portrait"
- H. P. Lovecraft's "The Outsider"
- Joyce Carol Oates's "The Artist"

Mathematics

This strategy works best for Mathematics when students are presented with a real-life problem that they solve either with a partner or independently, and then the teacher posts three potential strategies in separate corners, with the fourth corner being "None of these." The teacher then has students stand in the corner that most represents how they solved the problem. For example, students are given the problem, "Annie has three rows of carrots in her garden and wants to plant four carrot plants in each row. How many carrot plants will Annie plant altogether?" The Four Corners would be the following:

- I drew a picture or used manipulatives to solve the problem.
- I added to solve the problem (either 3 + 3 + 3 + 3 or 4 + 4 + 4).
- I multiplied to solve the problem.
- None of these.

Science

This example is a question that could be used in Science:

> Scientists are working on using gene splicing to potentially bring back extinct species. To what extent do you agree or disagree with scientists pursuing this endeavor?

- Strongly agree
- Somewhat agree
- Somewhat disagree
- Strongly disagree

Social Studies

This example is a question that could be used in Social Studies:

> To what extent do you agree with the decision to use the atomic bomb on Hiroshima near the end of World War II?

- Strongly agree
- Somewhat agree
- Somewhat disagree
- Strongly disagree

World Languages

This example is a question that could be used in World Languages:

> If you won a free vacation to anywhere in the world, which Spanish-speaking country would you visit? Be ready to justify your answer with examples of history, arts, food, and other cultural aspects.

- Spain
- Mexico
- Argentina
- Costa Rica

Music

This example is a question that could be used in Music:

> Using the performance competition rubric that will be used at our next competition, how would you rate our practice today? Be ready to justify your choice by citing tone quality, intonation, technique, and rhythm.

- Score of A
- Score of B
- Score of C
- Score of D

Visual Arts

This example is a question that could be used in Visual Arts:

To what extent do you agree with the following statement? "Advertisers should be allowed to digitally alter photographs and videos to better represent their products."

- Strongly agree
- Agree
- Disagree
- Strongly disagree

Health/Physical Education

This example is a question that could be used in Health or P.E.:

Which of the following circuit training plans would you most prefer to follow to keep in shape? Be ready to explain why using current research.

- Squats 3 × 10, Deadlifts 3 × 10, Rows 3 × 10,
- Bench Press 3 × 10, Lunges 3 × 10, Military Press 3 × 10
- Jumping Jacks 60 seconds, Mountain Climbers × 10, Squats × 10, Burpees × 10
- Bicep curls 3 × 10, Crunches 3 × 15, Leg Curl 3 × 10

Library/Media

This example is a question that could be used in Library/Media:

> For your upcoming research paper, with which resource will you start? Be ready to explain how the particular resource best suits your topic.

- Online encyclopedia
- Peer-reviewed journals
- Blogs/opinion articles
- Newspapers or similar

Career and Technical Education

This example question could be used for assessing problem-solving skills in real-life situations:

> You and a colleague are creating a website for your business together. You realize one evening that your colleague has been using narratives and pictures from other websites without permission in much of his work. It will take multiple days to fix the work. Which of these actions do you take?

- Contact my boss immediately
- Wait 24 hours to make a decision (knowing that he will continue working during this time)
- Confront my colleague using "I statements"
- Another strategy

The Task from Start to Finish

Identify

Franz Toban teaches elementary Music. He has been working with his first-grade students on fast and slow rhythms, high and low pitches, and how music can evoke an emotional response. He decides to use the Four Corners activity with his students to assess their understanding of these topics.

Plan

Franz looks up his district's standards for music, which include:

- Students will identify high and low pitches in music.
- Students will identify fast and slow rhythms in music.
- Students will describe their own emotional responses to music.

Phrase	Cognitive Process Dimension Category	Reasoning
Students will identify high and low pitches in music. Students will identify fast and slow rhythms in music.	Remember	In both of these, students are retrieving their knowledge of what high and low and fast and slow sound like to identify elements of pieces of music.
Students will describe their own emotional responses to music.	Understand	According to Anderson and colleagues (2001), one of the Cognitive processes for the Understand level is Explaining, which "occurs when a student is able to construct and use a cause-and-effect model of a system." Because students are listening to music (the cause), and identifying the effects (their emotions) by describing them, they are working at the Understand level.

Franz decides to use the Four Corners strategy to formatively assess his students on these topics.

Apply

Franz puts up four signs around the room in different corners: Happy, Sad, Angry, Other. The happy, sad, and angry signs also have pictures of an emoji that depicts that emotion. Franz tells students he will play a clip of music and students should think about whether they hear more high or low pitches and more fast or slow rhythms and how the song makes them feel. He then plays a clip from the opening of Dvorak's Symphony No. 9 "From the New World"–II–Largo. He points out the various signs up in the room and asks students to move to the corner that best describes how they felt when they heard the music.

Once they are there, he asks students to do a think-pair-share with a partner about whether the clip used a fast or slow rhythm and mostly high or low pitches while he walks around and listens to their conversations. He then facilitates a class discussion over what students heard and how it influenced what they felt.

Assess

Franz notes that students move as follows:

Emotional Corner	Number of Students	Stated Reasons during Discussion
Angry	0	N/A
Happy	5	"The song has higher pitches which seem happy." –John "I really liked it." –Monique "It makes me happy." –Gwenn
Sad	11	"The rhythm was really slow." –Kassidy "It sounds like a funeral song." –Vince "I think someone died." –Justice
Other	2	"It made me feel peaceful." –Grover "It was slow and made me sleepy." –Germany

From both his informal observations of their conversations and the classroom discussion, Franz notes that while some of his students (John, Kassidy, Germany) make note of either the pitch or the rhythm to justify their emotional response, most simply describe the emotion. Others (Monique, Gwenn) appear to have conflated liking something with it evoking a happy response.

Based on these results, Franz decides he will need to keep working with his students on helping them to identify how elements of music help to create various emotional responses. He also decides that for the next three class periods, he will play a clip of music at the beginning and model for students how to explain the musical elements that contribute to the emotional response, and then give the students an opportunity to listen to a different clip and do a think-pair-share on a similar topic. At the end of the three class periods, he will again assess students using the Four Corners activity.

Refine

Franz decides when he next uses the Four Corners strategy, he will keep a quick checklist of all his students like so:

Student Name	Emotion	Explains Emotion by Using Terms Involving Pitch	Explains Emotion by Using Terms Involving Rhythm

10 | Give One, Get One, Trade!

Description

Each student is given a notecard. He or she writes a review question on a given topic on the front and puts the answer (or an example of an answer) and a hint on the back. The teacher should review the question beforehand to ensure students write appropriate questions and have a clear understanding of the answer themselves.

Students stand up and walk around the classroom. When the teacher indicates for them to stop, they pair up with someone near them. One person reads the question and the other person attempts to answer. If the second person cannot answer, the first person reads the hint. If the second person still cannot answer, the first person quickly explains the answer. Then they switch, and work through the second person's question and card. At the end, they trade cards.

Students then walk around the classroom again, stop when the teacher says, and go through the process again with another student. The teacher can have students work with as many partners as desired.

Category of Cognitive Process Dimension

The questions have discrete answers and they work best with the Remember through Analyze levels. Teachers can also work with students on how to write questions at the Evaluate level, such as "Which president do you think has had the most positive effect on advancing civil rights in the United States and why?"

Learning Management

While this task can become a classroom staple, it requires some advance management on the part of the teacher. Even with older students, the teacher will want to model how to walk around the classroom carefully. The teacher will need to remind students to write neatly, as they will be trading their cards with other students.

Students will sometimes also struggle to find someone with whom to partner. One way to ensure they partner quickly is to do a Hand Up–Pair Up. When asked to stop walking, students raise one hand, "high five" someone next to them, and put their hand down. It is then easy for students to see who else still needs to pair up. Another technique is to have students who still need to pair up go to the front of the classroom, where they can quickly find others in need of partners.

Lastly, sometimes it is helpful to give musical or visual clues to students to indicate when to walk and when to stop. For instance, the teacher can play music while students are walking and turn it off when students should pair up. Similarly, the teacher can flash the lights on and off when students should stop walking.

Using the Data Effectively

The teacher will want to review all students' questions and answers before the students begin to share to determine who still has misconceptions. The teacher will also want to monitor informally to see who struggles with answers and explaining concepts to others.

Modifying and Differentiating the Strategy

The teacher can use pictures for students who are not strong readers/writers. In a pre-kindergarten classroom, for example, the teacher might give all students a picture of an animal on the front of a card and the letter that the animal's name starts with on the back of the card.

Examples by Subject

English Language Arts

Students can write examples of sentences with incorrect grammar and ask each other to edit them, or create questions based upon recent readings.

Mathematics

Students write math problems for one another and ask each other to determine the answer or the solution steps.

Science

Students can write example experiments and have each other identify elements such as hypotheses, independent, or dependent variables. Students can also write potential scientific questions for each other and then discuss how they would design an experiment to test or simulation or model to solve a problem.

Social Studies

The teacher can have students sequence events in history, write true-or-false questions, or determine cause-and-effects of events.

World Languages

Students can ask each other questions in the language being studied and practice answering in the language as well.

Music

Students can give each other examples of musical concepts, such as allegro, or 4:4 time, and other students either have to sing or play the concept.

Visual Arts

Students can ask each other questions about artistic techniques or time periods, or even ask questions about prints or other pieces of art.

Health/Physical Education

Students can write questions to review units on physical fitness, nutrition, or other health topics.

Library/Media

Students can write questions that require each other to find resources in the library (allow more time for this kind of hands-on question), scenarios involving digital citizenship, or questions about using technology.

Career and Technical Education

Questions reviewing for certification, and making business or life choices are examples of topics that students can write for one another.

 # The Task from Start to Finish

Identify

Gisella Frederick teaches French I in a Virginia high school. Her class is mostly composed of ninth graders who have had little or no exposure to the French language previously. She is at the end of her first unit, in which students have learned simple greetings and other sentences.

Plan

Gisella reviews the Virginia Department of Education standards for this unit:

FI.1 The student will exchange simple spoken and written information in French.

1. Use basic greetings, farewells, and expressions of courtesy both orally and in writing.

2. Express likes and dislikes, requests, descriptions, and directions.

3. Ask and answer questions about familiar topics.

Phrase	Category of Cognitive Process Dimension	Reasoning
FI.1 The student will exchange simple spoken and written information in French. 1. Use basic greetings, farewells, and expressions of courtesy both orally and in writing. 2. Express likes and dislikes, requests, descriptions, and directions. 3. Ask and answer questions about familiar topics.	Apply	In all of these, students are applying their knowledge to real-time conversations.

She decides to use the Give One, Get One, Trade! task to have students practice asking and answering questions about familiar topics.

Apply

There are 20 students in Gisella's French I class. She gives each student an example of a question they have to write, so that five students must ask a question about likes versus dislikes, five must ask for a request, five must ask for a description, and five must ask for a direction. She has them write down their questions on notecards, then she reviews them beforehand and helps students reword for grammar.

She then has students engage in the Give One, Get One, Trade! activity while she monitors and collects information. She makes sure to listen to each student at least once during the conversation.

Assess

During the activity, Gisella keeps the following chart:

Student	Grammar, Correctness	Grammar, Sophistication	Pronunciation
Eamon	3	3	3
Donte	1	1	2
Gus	2	2	1
Arya	3	2	2
Kiley	2	2	2
Jeanne	1	1	1
Africa	2	1	2
Nicolas	1	1	2
Mary-Grace	2	2	1
Lark	3	1	2
Evan	2	2	2
Sylvie	3	3	3
Mitchell	2	2	2
Mariah	1	2	1
AVERAGE	2.0	1.71	1.86
MODE	2	1	2

1 = Needs Significant Work

2 = Fair

3 = Great!

What Gisella notes is that, in general, her class tends to do best with using correct grammar, but the sophistication of the grammar is the lowest score. She interprets this to mean that students are choosing easier grammar and simpler replies to avoid making mistakes. Similarly, she notes that the most common score for sophistication of grammar is a 1, whereas the correctness of grammar and fluency both have most common scores of 2.

To that end, Gisella notes she will work with students on pushing themselves to increase the sophistication of their grammar and provide them with more opportunities like this one to practice.

Refine

Gisella would like to be able to give students opportunities to have conversations like this more often and collect more information on their ability to converse with one another. She therefore decides to do this task once a week so that she can keep a record of student progress.

11 | Graffiti Art

  ## Description

This formative assessment activity can be done as either a pre-assessment or at the end of a lesson (or both).

Take two giant pieces of butcher paper, such as the kind often used on bulletin boards. This is your "wall." Lay the paper on the floor, tables, or rows of desks. Divide students into two groups and provide markers. Give students the lesson topic and have them do a quick (three minutes or less) "graffiti" that displays their understanding of the topic. This can be a few words or phrases, a short poem, a comic, an illustration—whatever. Make sure students "tag" their work with either their initials or their name.

Next, have students switch "walls" so they can see what the other group did. Each student should respond to at least one other person's graffiti in some format (either a picture or maybe a few words of agreement or something else to consider)—and "tag" their response (total time: about three minutes). Then, students return to their original "wall" to see responses.

Next, have a discussion (either whole group, small group, or both) where students compare/contrast the work they saw on each Graffiti Wall. For older students, teachers can ask, "What overarching themes did you see? How did Wall 1 compare/contrast with Wall 2? What graffiti particularly struck you?" For younger students, teachers can ask, "What kinds of things did you see more than once on both walls? What did you see by someone else that you really liked?" The discussion should take about 7–10 minutes.

It is recommended that students with advanced-enough writing abilities also submit the answer to one or more questions on a notecard or scrap sheet of paper.

Category of Cognitive Process Dimension

This task works best for standards at the Remember and Understand level, though this formative assessment can possibly give insights into Application. The activity itself uses Analysis skills to compare/contrast the two "walls."

Through manipulation of the topic, the teacher could potentially ratchet up to even higher standards; for example, students might be given the topic "The Best President" (Social Studies). Another way to increase the rigor is to give each group specific prompts when moving from one "wall" to the other. For instance, in Science, students might be given the initial prompt: "Design an experiment to show if sound waves travel through water—note the independent and dependent variable." When students switch, they can then be given the prompt: "Add a materials list and explain what needs to be controlled in the proposed experiment."

Learning Management

The teacher will need to demonstrate to students how to carefully move around the graffiti paper and find a section on which to draw. The teacher might also need to explain to students that the marker color does not matter as much as getting their ideas on paper.

Using the Data Effectively

If used for pre-assessment, the activity can provide the teacher with ideas about student prior knowledge and possible misconceptions. If used at the end of a lesson, it can provide the teacher with a summary of the "big ideas" that students take away from the topic.

Modifying and Differentiating the Strategy

Students who do not have strong writing skills can be encouraged to draw pictures and explain them orally. They can also use pre-cut images or stickers to portray their learning.

Examples by Subject

We have provided content topics that can be used with this formative assessment activity.

English Language Arts

Author's Purpose

Mathematics

Finding Volume

Science

Cell Parts

Social Studies

The Pilgrims

World Languages

Words You Need When You Travel

Music

Tempo

Visual Arts

The Illusion of Space

Health/Physical Education

The FITT Principle (Frequency, Intensity, Time, and Type)

Library/Media

Inferences

Career and Technical Education

Workplace Readiness

The Task from Start to Finish

Identify

Tamara Jenks is a sixth-grade Mathematics teacher who is about to teach a unit on Statistics and Probability. While the students often do well on this section of their standardized assessment, Tamara knows they tend to think Statistics and Probability are all about applying formulas to a data set to determine median and/or mean, ranges, and deviations. She wants to start the unit by making sure that students understand the nature of Statistics and therefore decides to do a quick formative assessment on the very basic term "Statistics" as a diagnostic tool to see what her students already understand and think about the topic.

Plan

Tamara pulls up the Common Core standards for sixth-grade Mathematics and uses this one for the activity:

CCSS.MATH.CONTENT.6.SP.A.1.   Recognize a statistical question as one that anticipates variability in the data related to the question and accounts for it in the answers. For example, "How old am I?" is not a statistical question, but "How old are the students in my school?" is a statistical question because one anticipates variability in students' ages.

Phrase	Cognitive Process Dimension Category	Reasoning
Recognize a statistical question as one that anticipates variability in the data related to the question and accounts for it in the answers.	Understand	For this particular standard, students have to be able to determine if a question is a statistical one, which gets at the heart of statistics. This is at the Understand level, because students have to be able to understand what statistical questions look like in order to determine whether a particular question is one.

Apply

Before beginning the unit, Tamara gets two giant pieces of butcher paper, one red and one blue, each about 10 feet long. She lays them down on the floor with packets of markers. When students enter, Tamara asks them to silently consider what comes to mind when asked the question, "What is Statistics?" Tamara explains students will be drawing "graffiti" on a "wall," and shows them the butcher paper. She also uses her projector and whiteboard to show them a few examples of graffiti that uses images, phrases, and poetry.

She has students number off by ones and twos; the ones go to the red paper and the twos go to the blue paper. She instructs students to take a marker at the butcher paper and add their graffiti that answers the question "What is Statistics?" Tamara encourages students to include real-life examples, and reminds the students to "tag" their work with their first name and last initial.

She gives students three minutes to create their work, then has the groups switch. They have three minutes to review what other students drew and three minutes to create a response to one other person's work, and they have to "tag" their response, as well.

Tamara then has students return to their seats to turn and talk with a shoulder partner about any similarities and themes they noticed.

Assess

During this think-pair-share, Tamara inspects the butcher paper carefully to come up themes on her own.

Here is what Tamara can interpret based on some of the inscriptions:

Inscription	Student	Inference about Student Understanding
IDK	Amara H.	Amara generally has high test scores in mathematics, but is lacking some fundamental knowledge about real-life applications.
Something That's about Averages and That's Sorta Easy	Jenna M.	Jenna is a very verbally advanced student who sometimes struggles in Mathematics; using narratives and having her write her thinking will probably help her understand the concepts better.
#'s !	Paul L.	Paul has had several low standardized test scores in the area of Mathematics and this basic understanding probably means he will need help both on the computation and the real-life application of principles
	William Y.	William is the star forward on the basketball team and it might work well to use sports examples to help motivate him and other sports-minded students, and help them understand the concepts.
Mean, Mode, Median	Barkley J.	Barkley knows basic vocabulary relating to statistics, but again does not show evidence of a working knowledge of real-life applications.

Given that the majority of students give very broad answers, Tamara knows she needs to especially emphasize the purpose of statistics and real-life applications. She will use multiple means to communicate and have students process, such as giving students opportunities to journal about their understanding. She will also make sure to include real-life examples during the unit, especially on sports.

Refine

Tamara decides she will conduct the same activity at the end of the unit, only she will have students write one or two sentences explaining their graffiti art and how it represents their understanding of the answer to the question "What is Statistics?" so she can better gauge their thinking. She will also save these original graffiti "walls" and have students compare/contrast their first graffiti art to their second.

Human Likert Scale

Description

The teacher posts a statement (usually controversial or opinion based) about the content and a double-headed horizontal arrow on the board. On the left side of the arrow, it says "Strongly Disagree" and on the right side, it says "Strongly Agree." The teacher explains to the students if they strongly disagree with the statement, they will stand all the way to the left side of the room; if they strongly agree, they will stand all the way to the right. Students can also stand anywhere in the middle showing the degree to which they disagree or agree.

Once the students are in position, the teacher then has students pair up and discuss their reasons for where they are standing. Students come up with a one-to-two-minute "stump speech" in which they try to persuade others in the room to join them where they are. For larger classes, the teacher might have larger groups (suggested maximum is five), or have the pairs then synthesize their stump speech with another pair. Students deliver their speeches, and then the teacher asks if anyone has been persuaded to move based on someone else's speech.

In addition to monitoring informally while students discuss, the teacher should then have students individually respond (usually in writing) to explain (1) where they stood the first time; (2) why; and (3) if they moved, and why or why not.

Category of Cognitive Process Dimension

The Human Likert Scale usually falls in the Evaluate level in Bloom's Revised Taxonomy (Anderson et al., 2001), though having students put together stump speeches (especially if done more formally) could be considered the Create level. The other levels (especially Remember, Understand, and Analyze) are strongly featured because they are necessary in order to be able to Evaluate appropriately.

This task can be used with standards even at lower levels, such as Remember or Understand, in order to intrigue and motivate students to dig deeper into the learning.

 Learning Management

If the students are not used to getting up and moving during class, it might be necessary to demonstrate to them the first time or two how to determine where in the room to stand. For students who are not used to collaborating with one another, it might be necessary to model how to have a quick conversation in which both people speak, affirming and building upon each other's ideas.

For students who are very reluctant to share, it might be helpful to try to this first with a non-content topic that students might find very motivating. For instance, "School should start later in the day," or "Schools should not give students homework," or "Students should be allowed to use personal devices in class as long as it is for schoolwork." These kinds of topics will certainly get almost every student up and ready to share opinions—and once they are used to sharing, it is often easier to coax them into discussing more content-related topics.

  Using the Data Effectively

The teacher can use the informal monitoring of student conversations, stump speeches, and the quick write that takes place afterwards to determine: (1) the basic content knowledge that students have (more content knowledge will usually be required for more sophisticated arguments); (2) misconceptions regarding both basic factual knowledge and generalizations; (3) the students' abilities to reason using factual knowledge.

Modifying and Differentiating the Strategy

For younger students, consider more opinion-based rather than controversial strategies. For instance, a Mathematics teacher might use the statement, "I think adding is important," and use students' justifications to determine who understands how to apply adding to real-life situations.

Students with limited writing ability can justify their thinking orally or with pictures rather than in writing.

Advanced students who have previously been exposed to the task can be encouraged to come up with statements about the topic themselves to use with classmates.

Examples by Subject

These examples are statements that could be used for the various subject areas.

English Language Arts

Romeo and Juliet is an example of true love.

Mathematics

All people should memorize customary metric conversions.

Science

Farmers should use only organic fertilizers.

Social Studies

The best defense against tyranny is an educated populace.

World Languages

Every American should know at least one other language.

Music

Musical preference is a product of nurture rather than nature.

Visual Arts

Whether an artist is recognized in his or her own time is irrelevant.

Health/Physical Education

We have a duty not only to exhibit responsible personal and social behaviors, but also to help others exhibit them, too.

Library/Media

Information that is shared on the Internet should be regulated to check for accuracy.

Career and Technical Education

Workplace skills are often more important than content knowledge.

The Task from Start to Finish

Identify

Heidi Brookman teaches seventh-grade Life Science. She is about to begin a unit on Living Systems Structures and Processes and feels this is a very important topic for her students to not only understand in terms of factual knowledge, but also be able to use this knowledge to think critically.

Plan

Heidi reviews the Next Generation Science Standards. She decides to use the Human Likert Scale activity as both a pre-assessment and a check for understanding for her students for the following standard:

Students who demonstrate understanding can

MS-LS1–5.   Construct a scientific explanation based on evidence for how environmental and genetic factors influence the growth of organisms. [Clarification Statement: Examples of local environmental conditions could include availability of food, light, space, and water. Examples of genetic factors could include large breed cattle and species of grass affecting growth of organisms. Examples of evidence could include drought decreasing plant growth, fertilizer increasing plant growth, different varieties of plant seeds growing at different rates in different conditions, and fish growing larger in large ponds than they do in small ponds.] [Assessment Boundary: Assessment does not include genetic mechanisms, gene regulation, or biochemical processes.]

Phrase	Cognitive Process Dimension Category	Reasoning
Construct a scientific explanation based on evidence for how environmental and genetic factors influence the growth of organisms.	Create	Students must create a scientific explanation by putting together evidence. In order to ensure that students are actually working at the Create level, it's important that Heidi not simply give the scientific explanations to students, but also provide specific opportunities for them to examine the evidence and construct their own explanations.

After unpacking this standard and considering how to best get students to construct explanations, Heidi decides to use the Human Likert Scale because it requires students to use evidence to evaluate a statement, with special emphasis on having students construct their arguments.

Apply

Before teaching the two-day lesson, Heidi uses the Human Likert Scale activity with the statement, "Farmers should be required to use organic fertilizers." She has students who disagree strongly stand to the far left of the classroom, and who agree strongly stand to the far right; students who are moderate can stand anywhere in the middle. She then has students pair up with someone near them and each share two reasons why they chose to stand where they are. She then has students return to their seats and write short justifications (two to four sentences) explaining why they chose to stand where they did.

Heidi then teaches the two-day lesson, during which students look at studies and data regarding the effects (both positive and negative) of both organic and industrial fertilizers, including how they influence plant growth. During the previous unit, Heidi had begun a whole-class experiment in which students grew beans using organic fertilizer, industrial fertilizer, and no fertilizer, and during this unit, she had students observe, document, and compare the results as part of their evidence.

To check for understanding at the end of the two-day lesson, Heidi has students repeat the Human Likert Scale. This time, she has students develop "stump speeches" in groups of four, explaining that the speech can be no longer than two minutes and needs to contain at least four facts from the lesson. After students deliver their stump speeches, she asks students to move if they feel they have been persuaded.

Afterwards, she then has students return to their seats and answer the following in their science journals:

1. To what extent do you agree with the statement "Farmers should be required to use organic fertilizers"? Answer in a paragraph that explains:

   a. The extent to which you agree or disagree

   b. At least four pieces of scientific evidence from the last two days

2. Did the extent to which you agreed with this statement change from the first time we did it until now? Answer in two to three sentences that explain why or why not.

3. Which of your classmates' stump speeches made the biggest impact on the extent to which you agree with the statement? Answer in two to three sentences that explain why.

Assess

During the first round of the Human Likert Scale, Heidi notes that 18 of her 24 students stand to the right side of the classroom, indicating that they agree with the statement, and 10 of those stood to the far right. She listens to their discussions and reviews their short justifications, scoring each one quickly using the following rubric.

	0	1	2	3
Sophistication of Argument (SA)	Little or no	Limited	Moderate	Well-developed
Content Knowledge (CK)	Little or no	Limited	Moderate	Well-developed

Here are some example justifications, how Heidi used them to determine student understanding, and how she scored each:

"I think organic is just better. I don't want germs in my body." (Shows a misconception about the effects of fertilizer, and Heidi makes sure to speak one-on-one to this student to clear it up the next day; scored as SA-0; CK-0.)

"We use mostly organic fertilizer in our garden out back. It's better for the environment." (Heidi determines that this shows a general lack of factual knowledge in order to make sophisticated conclusions; scored this SA-0, CK-0.)

"I know that regular fertilizer can help plants grow better but my dad says that we pay some farmers not to grow food because we have too much. Maybe using only organic fertilizer would help that and our government could save money." (Shows slightly more sophistication than the earlier arguments, but is still missing key important factual knowledge and shows some misconception; scored as SA-1, CK-1.)

"I'm really torn. Organic is better because it puts less salt into the soil so the soil is more healthy, but it can cost a lot of money and I've read that most fertilizers aren't that bad for you." (Shows some prior knowledge and approaching sophistication; scored as SA-2, CK-2.)

"I remember from fourth grade that chemical fertilizer can wash down into the bay and cause more algae to grow, which is bad for the fish and plants in the water. I don't know if organic is the same but I bet it's better." (Shows some prior knowledge and approaching sophistication— and an understanding that the student knows what she doesn't know; scored as SA-2; CK-2.)

Heidi uses this information to put students into pairs for the exploration portions of the next two days of lessons. She tries to pair students so that weaker students work with stronger students, and also so that students are working with someone within one point of themselves on either Sophistication of Argument or Content Knowledge so that the difference in readiness levels does not frustrate students.

Because most students showed a preference for organic fertilizers but could not provide significant justification for why, Heidi makes sure she emphasizes the pros and cons of organic fertilizers during the course of the lesson.

After the two days of lessons and the second Human Likert Scale, Heidi uses the same rubric when reviewing students' science journals. She compares the scores for each student, and uses the information to determine who continues to need work on both the content knowledge and argument sophistication. Those who need more content knowledge are put into a review group before the summative assessment specifically on this material, and during the next group of lessons, Heidi checks in more frequently with those who need work on argument sophistication.

Refine

Heidi quickly polled her students to see how they liked the Human Likert Scale by having them hold up fingers on one hand (0 = Let's Never Do This Again; 5 = I Loved It). Most students held up four or five fingers, with a smattering of threes. When Heidi questioned the whole group, students explained they liked getting up out of their seats and the initial prompt made them want to learn more about the topic. She decides she will do this activity again, but next time she will also have students self-assess using the rubric, both on the pre-assessment and after the lesson.

Professional Development Plan
Movement Tasks

 Step 1

Read the chapter in advance of meeting as a group. Encourage colleagues to reflect on their own experiences in moving during professional development sessions versus those sessions that required a more "sit and get" approach. Prompt participants in advance of meeting to consider the following questions:

- What professional development activities used movement as a central part of the learning activities? What professional development did not?

- How did the Movement activities help you better learn the content of the session versus those sessions where you sat passively?

- What types of Movement activities had the most impact on your own learning? Did you use any of those Movement strategies within your own teaching? How?

   These questions draw on teachers' own experiences in faculty learning sessions, rather than those in their own instructional settings as teachers. This helps contextualize for the learning community the power of movement. A second iteration of this professional development plan can involve Movement questions within their own instructional classroom settings. We encourage you to start with prompting about the learning experiences of the adults to help anchor this professional development plan.

Step 2

In a face-to-face professional development session that is approximately one hour in length:

- Use the Human Likert Scale activity with the following prompt: "It is the responsibility of schools to ensure students move frequently throughout the day." Follow the directions in the Human Likert Scale section have participants share and debate.

- Put participants in groups of four (either heterogeneous or with like grade levels/subject areas). Have each group discuss the following reflection questions:
  - What are the benefits to movement in the classroom?
  - What are some of the challenges you potentially see regarding using movement in your classroom? How might you overcome them?
  - Which task can most likely see yourself implementing in the classroom over the next week?
  - How will you review the data and what instruction decisions do you anticipate yourself making?

- Give participants this task: "Use at least one of the Movement formative assessment techniques in your class over the next week and be ready to discuss how it went." Optional: require participants to try out two of the tasks.

- Do a Graffiti Art mural with participants either writing a pithy saying or drawing a picture to show which task they will use.

Step 3

Conduct walkthroughs as staff implement the formative assessment strategies over the next week. Consider collaborative walkthroughs as well as individual peer walkthroughs.

Step 4

In a follow-up face-to-face professional development session approximately one hour in length:

- Review the topic with a Four Corners. In four separate corners, post the names of various rides from an amusement park (suggested: roller coaster, Ferris wheel, bumper cars, teacups). Give participants the prompt: which amusement park ride *best* represents the task you tried out went? Allow 30 seconds to consider, then have participants move to the appropriate corner. In the corner, they should find a partner and explain why they chose that corner. Monitor while the pairs discuss, and then call on participants from each corner to explain their reasoning to the whole group. Use the information to help guide the discussion through the rest of the professional development session.

- Give each participant a notecard and have him or her write down one idea for a subject/topic during which a Movement task can be used. Make sure participants write out the topic, the Movement task, and useful tips they found for implementing the task. Use the Give One, Get One, Trade strategy.

- Put participants in groups of four (either heterogeneous or with like grade levels/subject areas). Have each group discuss the following reflection questions:

  - What task did you try? What worked well? What might you do differently next time?

  - What instructional decisions did you make based on the task?

  - How will you use this professional development to make a change in your practice that positively impacts your students and their achievement?

- Revisit the Graffiti Art mural and have participants add to their original designs, then discuss what they noticed as similarities and differences between the mural depictions.

Select Response: Formative Assessment Strategies

Integrating Select Response into Formative Assessments

Select Response assessments, in which the teacher provides a set of potential responses and the students choose the best one, have always been popular in K–12 classrooms, and that popularity has only increased in recent years. Standardized multiple choice assessments, online technologies with Select Response formats, and the like have made it both easier and more imperative to teach students how to answer Select Response items. In addition to multiple choice, Select Response items are usually either matching or true/false in construction (Gareis & Grant, 2008).

There are other benefits to Select Response items, of course. They can be graded quickly and with little subjectivity. A teacher does not need to ponder the degree to which an answer is correct; the student has either chosen the correct answer(s) or has not. In terms of providing formative assessment, a few well-written Select Response items allow teachers to provide rapid feedback to students. Also, because of the lack of subjectivity in these types of items, the teacher can quickly sort students into groups for enrichment or remediation based on the data yielded by these Select Response assessments.

Of course, there are drawbacks to using Select Response. When teachers provide answers and students choose the best one, it can be hard to know whether the student actually *knows* the answer, is guessing, or something in the construction of the item gave the student an unintentional clue. In assessment terms, this is called a threat to reliability. In *Teacher Made Assessments: How to Connect Curriculum, Instruction, and*

Student Learning (2008), Gareis and Grant write that teachers want to ask themselves:

> Did the student answer a question correctly because he truly knew the answer and nothing in the item gave the answer away? Conversely, did the student answer a question incorrectly because he truly did not know the answer and something in the item did not confuse the students to the point that, even though he knew the correct answer, he chose an incorrect answer.
>
> (2008, p. 92)

Some teachers might say that using clues in poorly constructed items to determine the correct answer is just good test-taking on the part of the students, but consider: Our goal here is to find out what our students actually *know* about the curriculum. Unless test-taking is an actual standard in your curriculum, you should make every effort to construct reliable test items rather than ones that confuse, trick, or help students (even if they are constructed that way unintentionally).

Another drawback of Select Response assessments is that, quite frankly, there are often limits to what these items can assess. While it is possible to write Select Response items that assess up to the Analyze level, these types of items often assess lower-level skills, such as those at the Remember and Understand levels. The Evaluate level requires students to make a decision and justify it, which can be difficult to do when students are merely choosing answers that are already given. Meanwhile, the Create level is virtually impossible when students are only being asked to select a predetermined answer.

This is not to say, however, that teachers should never use Select Response to formatively assess students when it comes to higher-level standards, such as those at the Evaluate or Create level. Indeed, sometimes the teacher needs to determine whether students remember and understand basic facts, or whether they can apply a basic process or formula, before having students move on to upper level tasks that require students to evaluate and create. Therefore, we do not advocate that teachers *never* use Select Response items to formatively assess students on standards that require higher-level skills, but rather that teachers be very purposeful in *why* he or she is using the Select Response assessment, and understand that other means of formative or summative assessment might be required to truly know whether the student has mastered the skill.

Tips for Using Select Response Tasks for Formative Assessment

- If using true/false items, make sure that the item is either completely true or completely false. In order to get a more accurate picture of what students understand, consider requiring students to underline any false information and correct it (Gareis & Grant, 2008).

- If using matching, provide an uneven number of matching items in each set, so that students will either use some items in one column more than once, or some items in a column will not be used at all. This will ensure that students cannot simply guess an answer through process of elimination (Gareis & Grant, 2008).

- For multiple-choice questions, ensure that all answer choices are plausible. Resist the urge to include "throwaway" answers that students can easily eliminate. Consider using fewer questions and asking students to justify their answers in order to get a truer picture of what students understand and eliminate the possibility of guessing (Gareis & Grant, 2008).

13 | ABC Cups

Description

This formative assessment works well as both a pre-assessment and throughout the lesson itself.

You will need three class sets of paper or plastic cups—one class set per color. (Hint: red, yellow, and green work really well and can be used for multiple purposes.) You can give each student, each pair, or each group a set that has each color in it. Note that for older students, you can add a fourth color. Mark one color with A (let's say green), one color with B (yellow), and one color with C (red).

When students enter the classroom, ask them a question with three potential answer choices, and let them know that one or more of the answers can be correct. For example:

Which of the following is/are true about George Washington? Choose ALL that apply and move the cup with the corresponding letter to the RIGHT of your desk.

A. He was the first president of the United States.

B. He was elected unanimously.

C. He was assassinated.

The teacher can easily see incoming student misconceptions and tailor the lesson to meet them. The teacher should designate certain checkpoints throughout the lesson for students to update their original choices by moving cups if necessary, and the teacher can use these checkpoints to determine who is "getting it" and whether individuals or the class as a whole can move on.

While pieces of colored construction paper can also be used, cups are recommended because they are more easily seen from the front of the classroom.

Category of Cognitive Process Dimension

Because this is a Select Response task, it can generally assess up to the Analyze level, depending on how the question is written.

Learning Management

The teacher will need to model and set procedures for appropriate use of the cups. For instance, the teacher might want to model how students should not look at their peers when determining where to move their cups. If students are using the cups in pairs or groups, the teacher will want to model how to have those on-task conversations that take both students' opinions into account.

Using the Data Effectively

This is an on-the-spot formative assessment that can be used to guide a lesson in the moment. It can be combined with an Exit Ticket on the same or a similar question in order to determine individual student understanding in more depth.

Modifying and Differentiating the Strategy

The cups can also later be used for independent work so that students who put a red cup on top "Need the teacher's assistance help right away to continue work"; those with a yellow cup "Need the teacher's assistance but can keep working in the meantime"; and a green cup on top means, "All is well; no assistance currently needed."

Another interesting idea is to have students rank choices using the cups instead of choosing correct answers.

Examples by Subject

These examples are questions and answers that could be used for the various subject areas.

English Language Arts

Which of the following are examples of similes?

A. His smile was as bright as the sun.

B. She talked a mile a minute.

C. He drank like a camel.

Mathematics

Which of the following does NOT equal 19 if $x = 8$?

A. $3x - 8$

B. $2x + 3$

C. $4x - 13$

Science

Which of the following are present in animal cells?

A. Nucleus

B. Mitochondria

C. Cell Wall

Social Studies

Which of the following was *not* a result of Reconstruction?

A. Freed African Americans needed food, clothing, and shelter.

B. Northern railroads and farms were destroyed.

C. Sharecropping became an important system in the South.

World Languages

Which of the following mean "large" in Spanish?

A. Importante

B. Numeroso

C. Amplio

Music

Which of these instruments is/are in the brass family?

A. Trombone
B. Trumpet
C. Saxophone

Visual Arts

Which of these is a primary color?

A. Red

B. Purple

C. Green

Health/Physical Education

Which of the following are rules in basketball?

A. Once the offensive team puts the ball in play behind the mid-court line, it has 10 seconds to move the ball over the mid-court line.

B. The ball is moved by dribbling and passing.

C. Free throws are worth two points.

Library/Media

Which genres of books do you enjoy reading?

A. Poetry

B. Fiction

C. Nonfiction

Career and Technical Education

Which of the following would be appropriate uses of business email?

A. You send an email notifying an employee that his job is being eliminated with a link to unemployment resources.

B. You send an email to your employees with a link to your little sister's wrapping paper fundraiser in case they want to buy some.

C. You send an email to a colleague asking about progress on a project with an upcoming deadline.

The Task from Start to Finish

Identify

Melia Richards teaches second grade and is going to teach on Earth events, including volcanic explosions, earthquakes, and mountain formation. She wants to determine her students' background information and to formatively assess their progress as they research volcanoes and earthquakes using provided books and websites. She decides to use the ABC Cup strategy to see if students know whether the aforementioned Earth events are generally considered "fast" or "slow" processes.

Plan

Melia unpacks the following standard:

2-ESS1–1: Use information from several sources to provide evidence that Earth events can occur quickly or slowly. [Clarification Statement: Examples of events and timescales could include volcanic explosions and earthquakes, which happen quickly and erosion of rocks, which occurs slowly.]

Phrase	Cognitive Process Dimension Category	Reasoning
Use information from several sources to provide evidence that Earth events can occur quickly or slowly.	Understand	The thrust of the standard is not simply that students are memorizing whether some events are faster or slower, but rather that they are using the cognitive process Infer in the Understand category, which means that they are drawing a logical conclusion from presented information.

Apply

At the start of Science, Melia hands each student the following cups: A (green), B (yellow), and C (red). She puts the following question on the board:

Which of the following happen QUICKLY? Move that cup to the front of your desk.

A. Volcanic explosions

B. Earthquakes

C. Mountain formation

Melia reads the question aloud to her class. She has students move cups to the front and back of their desks because some students still struggle with left/right and she does not want that to interfere with the validity of the formative assessment.

Assess

Melia notes the following breakdown of her 23 students at the beginning of the lesson:

Type of Earth Event	Number of Students Who Say It Happens Quickly	Number of Students Who Say It Happens Slowly
Volcanic explosion	19	4
Earthquake	13	10
Mountain formation	8	15

Melia puts her students into pairs and provides several materials, including library books with specific passages marked and student-friendly websites and videos linked on her class website. She has done similar research lesson with her students before, so they are familiar with working in pairs to review materials. She provides each student with a graphic organizer to help guide the work.

Melia knows she needs to pay special attention to students when they work on the earthquake and mountain formation section of their research. Therefore, she tends to hover more frequently near the earthquake and mountain formation materials because she has organized the materials for each type of Earth event in different areas of the room,

Halfway through their research, Melia has students return to their seats and revisit their cups, moving them if they find it necessary. She takes another quick count and sees the following:

Type of Earth Event	Number of Students Who Say It Happens Quickly	Number of Students Who Say It Happens Slowly
Volcanic explosion	23	0
Earthquake	18	5 (Lucas, Amily, Tilda, Jackson, Reese)
Mountain formation	17	6 (Lucas, Amily, Tilda, Jackson, Veronica, Jim)

This time, Melia targets the students who still have one or more answers incorrect and works with them specifically to help them find the correct answers and understand.

At the end of the class, Melia gives her students one last opportunity to move their cups and has the following results:

Type of Earth Event	Number of Students Who Say It Happens Quickly	Number of Students Who Say It Happens Slowly
Volcanic explosion	23	0
Earthquake	22	1 (Lucas)
Mountain formation	22	1 (Amily)

Melia meets with Lucas and Amily again to review specifically with them while the rest of the students clean up.

Refine

Melia decides that next time she will also have the students use the cups as an indicator of when they need help by changing them from green to either yellow or red when they need assistance.

Entrance Tickets

 ## Description

Entrance Tickets can be used for multiple purposes to gather information as students enter a classroom. While they can be Supply Response items, in this case, we are going to describe how to use them as a Select Response strategy where teachers give students potential answer choices and use their selections to make decisions about lessons "on-the-spot."

 ## Category of Cognitive Process Dimension

This formative assessment activity work best for Remember to Analyze levels because we are using these as Select Response tickets.

 ## Learning Management

The teacher will need to establish routines for answering the Entrance Tickets. For instance, perhaps the teacher stands and greets students at the door and hands them an Entrance Ticket. Perhaps students know to grab an Entrance ticket on their way to their seats. Routines for device usage upon entry to the classroom need to be established for those teachers choosing to use a digital Entrance Ticket.

Using the Data Effectively

The teacher can use the information from the entrance ticket in multiple ways:

- Determine student preferences or interests in relation to the content.
- Assess student prior knowledge about a topic.
- Assess student understanding of the content.
- Assess student completion of independent work (such as homework or flipped classroom assignments).

 ## Modifying and Differentiating the Strategy

Students can be given different Entrance Tickets depending on readiness levels. Very young students or English Language Learners can be given Entrance Tickets using visual aids or pictures.

 # Examples by Subject

English Language Arts

Entrance Tickets on themes, story events, or other information from assigned reading all work well for this strategy.

Mathematics

While straight computation can be useful for determining students' skills, using word problems helps to determine whether students understand how to apply concepts in real-world situations.

Science

Questions can focus on factual information needed for the day, but can also assess student understanding of scientific design processes, such as the independent/dependent variable in a given experiment, and how to make an experiment more rigorous.

Social Studies

Entrance Tickets can be used as diagnostic tools to determine prior knowledge on a given topic or to determine student understanding from previously completed lessons.

World Languages

Entrance Tickets may ask students to translate phrases to/from English or focus on cultural information.

Music

The teacher could play a short piece of music and then ask students to circle the stanza that shows what was played.

Visual Arts

The teacher might ask students to match works of art with their time period and select true facts about an artist's life.

Health/Physical Education

Entrance Tickets might feature questions on consequences of drug use, nutritional information, or elements of physical fitness.

Library/Media

Entrance Tickets could be used to determine what students already know about library procedures, to give them a question they have to answer by looking up a book in the online catalog or using a particular resource, or to find out their prior knowledge about using/citing sources.

Career and Technical Education

Students can answer questions regarding knowledge of personal finance, interests that might help them determine a personal business, or prior information about food handling, etc.

The Task from Start to Finish

Identify

Leon Marcus teaches 12th-grade English and is embarking on one of his more challenging but favorite pieces of literature, *Waiting for Godot*. It was assigned as summer reading for his students and he is excited to work through the text with students. He will also be exploring one of the more challenging skills for his students: identifying inferences from the text.

Plan

Leon reviews the Common Core Reading standards for this unit:

CCSS.ELA-LITERACY.RL.11–12.1.   Cite strong and thorough textual evidence to support analysis of what the text says explicitly as well as inferences drawn from the text, including determining where the text leaves matters uncertain.

Phrase	Cognitive Process Dimension Category	Reasoning
Cite strong and thorough textual evidence to support analysis of what the text says explicitly as well as inferences drawn from the text, including determining where the text leaves matters uncertain.	Analyze	Standard, students must break the text into parts (explicitly stated information versus inferences versus what is left uncertain) in order to determine how the parts relate to an overall structure or purpose, and are therefore working at the Analyze level.

Before comparing explicit information versus inferences versus what the text leaves uncertain, Leon first wants to know whether students can make inferences—and also whether they completed the text as expected.

He therefore decides that on the day he will be reviewing *Waiting for Godot* with students, he will begin by giving them an Entrance Ticket that can both assess their abilities to recognize inferences and whether they read the play.

Apply

As students enter, Leon gives them the following Entrance Ticket:

Based upon your reading, which of the following is an inference that can be drawn from reading Waiting for Godot? Choose all that apply.

A. Estragon's final despair and decision to end his own life and leave Vladimir alone implies that the only escape from the mundaneness of human existence is an ultimate escape and that you must be both brave and cowardly to pursue it before it pursues you.

B. The repetitive and tiresome dialogue is meant to bore the audience in the same way that Estragon and Vladimir confront boredom; the audience, like the characters, feels bidden to stay in a way that can be seen as representative of the mundaneness of human existence.

C. The main characters' inability to remember their own pasts, the sparse setting, and the indistinct passage of time are all important aspects of the play.

Answer A is an interesting example of an inference—interesting because it does not actually occur in the text. Students who choose this answer can identify inferences but did not read the play (or even a synopsis on the Internet). Answer C is true about the play but is not an example of an inference. Students who choose answer B most likely can both identify an inference *and* have actually read the play.

Assess

As students enter, Leon has the question posted on the board. Students know to answer silently, write their answer on a sticky note, and turn it over until Leon collects it. As he collects the sticky notes, he finds the following information.

Group	Answer Choices	Implication	Students
1	B only	Read play; understands inferences	Deidre, Anna, Trinity, Zion, Tabitha, Kevin, Justin, Lillian, Joaquin
2	C only OR B and C	Read play; doesn't understand inferences	Maria, Diego, Philip, Michael, Evelyn
3	A and B	Didn't read play; understands inferences	Francis, Shelby
4	A only OR A and C OR A, B, and C	Didn't read play; doesn't understand inferences	Horatio, Emily

Leon has students in Group 1 immediately begin working on an activity in which they dive into teasing apart inference, explicitly stated information, and what is left uncertain around a theme. For those students in Group 2, he pulls them into a small group to do a quick review on inferences.

For students in Groups 3 and 4, Leon meets with them to discuss whether they read or finished the play, and when they acknowledge that they did not, he gives them time during class to read and explains they will be expected to do some of the classwork for homework or come work with him after school or during their lunch periods.

Refine

A couple of the students complain they thought that because the question said "Choose all that apply," they thought they had to choose more than one answer. Leon decides he needs to work with the students on thinking critically and developing test-taking skills in addition to working on specific English content.

Exit Tickets

 ## Description

Exit Tickets are a great way to see what students know at the end of a period of instruction. While they can be in a Supply Response format, here we will detail how to use them by giving students responses to choose from.

At the end of the lesson, the teacher gives students Select Response items (usually one to four items) on the material learned during that period. Students choose the correct answers and the teacher uses the information to make future instructional decisions.

 ## Category of Cognitive Process Dimension

This Select Response strategy works best with the Remember through Analyze levels.

 ## Learning Management

The teacher should explain the expectations for completing the Exit Ticket beforehand, such as whether students may speak or use their notes and how they turn in the ticket.

Using the Data Effectively

The teacher can use the information to make either whole-class decisions (for instance, to determine areas that the majority of the class needs to review) or individual decisions.

Modifying and Differentiating the Strategy

Younger students can complete an Exit Ticket that is mostly picture-based with simple, oral instructions from the teacher. (For instance: "Circle the picture of an object whose name starts with the letter B.")

Examples by Subject

These examples are questions and answers that could be used for the various subject areas.

English Language Arts

Which of the following is an example of an opinion?

A. Vanilla flavoring comes from an orchid plant.

B. Vanilla flavoring is used in foods such as ice cream, frosting, etc.

C. Vanilla is the second-most expensive spice after saffron.

D. Vanilla is the best flavor.

Mathematics

Which of the following shows how four cookies can be divided equally by two people?

Choice 1	
Greg	Madeline
○ ○	○ ○
Choice 2	
Greg	Madeline
○ ○ ○	○

Science

Which of the following is not a renewable energy source?

A. Wind

B. Water

C. Coal

D. Sunlight

Social Studies

Match the following people with their accomplishments. NOTE: People may be used more than once or not at all.

People	Accomplishments
_____Known as the Father of Our Country _____Known at the Father of the Constitution _____Wrote the Declaration of Rights _____Commander-in-Chief of the Continental Army _____Third President of the United States	Thomas Jefferson James Madison George Washington Patrick Henry

World Languages

"Etcetera" translates to—

A. And the rest

B. In other words

C. For example

D. On the other hand

Music

Which of the following was NOT a composer during the Baroque period?

A. Handel

B. Beethoven

C. Vivaldi

D. Bach

Visual Arts

In Adobe Photoshop, using the History palette allows you to:

A. Save your work in multiple formats

B. Share your work with other collaborators

C. Delete a series of steps used in a graphic design

D. Select an abnormally shaped image in a layer

Health/Physical Education

Label each example as either a sedentary lifestyle (SL) or active lifestyle (AL):

___Clara works all in day in an office at her desk and goes home and watches television.

___Chuck works as a furniture mover and goes swimming afterward most days.

___Rayna is a ballet dancer during the day and at night sings in a jazz band.

___Ben is a computer programmer during the day and at night plays basketball four times a week.

Library/Media

Which website would most likely give you information on how chewing gum is manufactured?

A. Chewing Gum | Definition of Chewing Gum

B. Chewing Gum (American Dental Association)

C. Make Chewing Gum at Home (Directions)

D. From the Factory to Your Mouth: Chewing Gum

Career and Technical Education

(Child Development:) Which of these is NOT a milestone that most babies experience in the first month?

A. Focuses on objects 8–12 inches away

B. Raises head when on stomach

C. Bangs and shakes objects

D. Makes fists with hands

 # The Task from Start to Finish

Identify

Shalamar Hopkins teaches a Career and Technical Education (CTE) high school Child Development course. She uses the Virginia CTE Resource

Center's Child Development competencies to plan her unit on Evaluating Parenting Practices That Maximize Human Growth and Development.

Plan

Shalamar refers to the following competency and unpacks it:

Distinguish among guidance, discipline, and punishment.

Phrase	Cognitive Process Dimension Category	Reasoning
Distinguish among guidance, discipline, and punishment.	Understand	Students are using the Compare cognitive process in the Understand level when they explain differences between and sort examples as guidance, discipline, or punishment.

Apply

Shalamar teaches a lesson on guidance, discipline, and punishment, including providing definitions and case studies for students to review and sort based on the definitions. She spends the day helping students to understand the definitions and examples of them, which is at the Understand level.

At the end of the lesson, she gives her students an Exit Ticket that consists of two questions related to the definitions, plus a third question to act as a "preview" to the next day's lesson at the Analyze level, so that she can use the information to help guide her lesson.

1. Setting and enforcing a bedtime for a child is an example of—

   A. Discipline

   B. Punishment

   C. Guidance

2. Taking away a child's cell phone because he stayed out too late is an example of—

   A. Discipline

   B. Punishment

   C. Guidance

3. Which of the following is least likely to teach leadership to children?

   A. Discipline

   B. Punishment

   C. Guidance

During the last five minutes of the class, Shalamar has her students complete the questions as part of an online Exit Ticket. After the class, she looks at the results, which follow.

	Question 1 (Review)	Question 2 (Review)	Question 3 (Preview)
Ricky	✓	✓	
Nevaeh	✓	A	
Nazir	✓	✓	✓
Ayisha	B	✓	
Che	✓	✓	✓
Kim	✓	✓	✓
Noah	✓	✓	
Ella	✓	A	
Jayden	✓	A	
Zoe	✓	✓	✓
Skylar	B	A	
Number of students who answered correctly (out of 11)	9	7	4

Note: Check marks indicate correct answers. Letters indicate which incorrect answer a student selected. Blank cells mean that the student did not answer that question.

What Shalamar notices a few students appear to be confusing Discipline and Punishment. She makes a note to more clearly define it the next day.

She also notices that four of her students (Nair, Che, Kim, and Zoe) were able to figure out the answer for Question 3, the preview question for the next day's lesson. She decides during the analysis project that students will complete the next day, she will have these four students work together so she can provide them with a more challenging prompt.

Refine

Shalamar decides that next time she will have students write a justification for their answers on the Preview question so she can determine whether they actually understand the answer they selected or are just guessing.

Question Hunt

  ## Description

This is a great way to do a Select Response activity that also gets students up, moving, and thinking.

Before the lesson the teacher places "question cards" in opaque containers (Easter eggs work well for this, but other containers, especially bigger ones, can work as well or better) and can either hide them around the classroom or another room to which the teacher has access.

Students can either work individually or in groups. The teacher gives students a set of one to five answer cards; the number can depend on the ability of the students.

Students then search around the room for the containers. When they find a container, they open it and check to see whether the question in it matches any of their answers. If it does, they take the container and put both the question and the answer in it. If it does not, they return the question to the container.

It is helpful if students check in with the teacher each time they think they have a matching question and answer; otherwise, students might hold the incorrect question and other students will not be able to complete their task.

To make things trickier, the teacher can include more question containers than there are answer cards.

Category of Cognitive Process Dimension

This activity tends to work best with the Remember and Understand categories, though depending on how the questions are written, could go up to the
Apply level (e.g., students might solve a math problem) or the Analysis level
(e.g., the question could be written so that students have to compare/con-
trast two concepts, as in "How are Concept A and Concept B" the same?")

Learning Management

Especially for younger or more impulsive students, the teacher will need to
model how to walk around the classroom, find containers, open containers, and put them back appropriately.

If the teacher does not want students going through certain areas, the
teacher should state ahead of time which places are "off limits" and do
not have any containers (for instance: the teacher might not want students
going into a personal desk or drawer).

Using the Data Effectively

If possible, the teacher should have the students check in after each time
they think they have a question that matches one of their answers. (It might
be helpful to label all the questions with a number and all the answers with
a letter, and then have an Answer Guide the teacher can glance at quickly.)
The teacher gives immediate feedback to students and corrects any misconceptions as students reveal them.

Modifying and Differentiating the Strategy

For non-readers, the teacher might choose to use more pictures than words.
Students can also be partnered with other students to provide more support, though it's recommended that students are not paired with someone
significantly above or below their current level, as that might lead to one
student doing all the work.

Examples by Subject

English Language Arts

This works well with vocabulary, characters and their descriptions, or stories and their elements.

Mathematics

This can be used with almost any topic in Mathematics in which students are given a set of answers or solutions and students must find the appropriate problems to match.

Science

This works well with vocabulary or factual knowledge and can also be used with diagrams. For instance, the teacher might include on the question card a picture of a cell with an arrow pointing to the mitochondria, and then create an answer card that explains the function of the mitochondria.

Social Studies

This can be used with vocabulary, dates, people, or events. For instance, the teacher might have the phrase "Not enough supply to meet the demand" on the answer card, and "What is scarcity?" on the matching question card.

World Languages

This works well with vocabulary. For instance, the teacher might have the Latin phrase "ab uno disce omnes" on the answer card, and "What Latin phrase means 'from one, learn all'?" on the question card.

Music

Students can find stanzas or lines of songs they are playing in Band or singing in Chorus and match them with the correct songs.

Visual Arts

Students can be given examples of famous artwork for their question cards and have to find the name of the artist in a question container. Students in graphic design courses might have the name of a particular process (such as "cropping an image") and have to find the directions for how to do that from a question container.

Health/Physical Education

Students can use this activity to match vocabulary words and definitions or rules to specific games or sports.

Library/Media

This task can be used as a lesson to get students used to the library, its layout and resources, and its policies. For instance, an answer might be, "One week," and the accompanying question would be, "For how long may a book be checked out?" Other questions might require students to perform tasks to discover the answers, such as "5" and the answer is "How many books by Roald Dahl does the library have?" If students are required to perform tasks, it is probably best not to give them a large set of answer cards or to let them work together.

Career and Technical Education

An Accounting teacher might use this to have students understand basic vocabulary words, such as "fiscal period," "work sheet," and "trial balance." Students would be given an answer card with the definition and then have to find the question that asks them to define the matching vocabulary word.

The Task from Start to Finish

Identify

Lula Jones is a kindergarten teacher. When she gives her beginning-of-year diagnostic assessments, she realizes the majority of her students are very low in being able to identify letters and their sounds. She works with students on the letters B, C, D, and F and decides to use the Question Hunt one day to test them.

Plan

Lula uses this Common Core Reading: Foundational Skills standard:

CCSS.ELA-LITERACY.RF.K.3.A   Demonstrate basic knowledge of one-to-one letter-sound correspondences by producing the primary sound or many of the most frequent sounds for each consonant.

Phrase	Cognitive Process Dimension Category	Reasoning
Demonstrate basic knowledge of one-to-one letter-sound correspondences by producing the primary sound or many of the most frequent sounds for each consonant.	Remember	It might seem like this is an Apply level skill (because students need to produce the primary sound for each consonant), but because the primary skill required is simply remembering the sound(s) made by each letter, it is more appropriate at the Remember level. When students begin to use the letter sounds to sound out words in text, it would the be more appropriate to consider it in the Apply level.

Apply

Because she has so many pre-readers, Lula decides her question cards will actually be pictures and her answer cards will be the letters B, C, D, and F. Each student will be given only one letter for their answer cards. She has 20 students, so five students get B, four students get C, etc. She hides 60 eggs in the garden outside, each with one picture of a word that starts with B, C, D, or F inside—15 pictures for each letter.

Each student is given a basket (a large plastic cup) they can use to collect their eggs once they think they have found one that matches their letter. If they open an egg that does not match their letter, they should put the letter back in the egg. Lula models both actions for students.

Because these are kindergarteners, Lula ensures her shared kindergarten assistant is with her, as well as the Special Education teacher with whom she co-teaches. Each student is assigned to a different adult as their "checker," and students are given the direction that whenever they think they have a match, they should check in with their assigned adult.

When a student has found three picture question cards that match her or his answer letter cards, and they have verified this through their assigned adult, they can play in the nearby playground.

Assess

After modeling the activity, Lula, the instructional assistant, and the Special Education teacher assist the students. The students bring them their eggs to be checked, and the adults each complete a chart for their assigned students that looks like the following.

Student(s)	Letter	Number of Incorrect Attempts	Incorrect Word(s)
Malaysia	B	0	
Sierra	C	|	cake (thought the picture was showing "bake")
Thomas	B	|||	duck, dog, dollar

Stephen	C	卌 ‖‖	dog, deer, desk, diamond, baby, banana, balloon, bat, fan

From this, Lula can see that Malaysia definitely has the sound for B down, as well as words that start with B. For Sierra, she sees that while Sierra had one incorrect attempt, it was a confusion over what was being depicted in the picture rather than not understanding the sounds. She determines that for the letters they had, neither girl needs remediation.

For Thomas, Lula notices all his incorrect attempts start with the letter D, even though he was given the letter B. She realizes Thomas is having difficulty distinguishing the "buh" sound from the "duh" sound, and will need to work with him on that.

Stephen, meanwhile, made several errors that appear to be random. Lula and the Special Education teacher later have a talk about how Stephen, who does not have an Individualized Education Program (IEP), has been struggling, and what next steps they should take to monitor and support him.

Refine

Lula's students really enjoyed the activity and said they would like to do it again one day. Lula decides that next time she will scaffold the learning so that some students (like Malaysia and Sierra) are given a second letter to search for after they find enough words that start with their first letter. She will also schedule the next session during a time when one or two of the fifth grade volunteers who come to her class once a week can be there to work one-on-one with Stephen.

Moreover, Lula decides she will use a mini-version of the Question Hunt during her reading groups so she can more precisely pinpoint which students know the sounds for which letters.

Professional
Development Plan
Select Response Tasks

Step 1

Read the chapter in advance of meeting as a group. Ask teachers to reflect on their own experiences with formative assessment strategies prior to coming to the professional development session. What do they know about formative assessments? What is the difference between formative and summative assessments?

Step 2

Before the meeting, develop a series of questions based around formative and summative assessment practices. A good text to use to develop your questions is *Formative Assessment Leadership: Identify Plan, Apply, Assess, Refine* (Sanzo, Myran, & Caggiano, 2015). You should also use materials provided through your school district around formative and summative assessment practices. These are the types of questions you would expect your colleagues to already know how to answer through previous professional development activities, and this session can serve as a refresher on the topics.

Before the session take opaque Easter eggs—or envelopes—that have some sort of identifiable marker that shows they are part of the professional development session and place one question in each egg, envelope, or other container. Put the containers around the professional development space—these can be hidden or out in the open. The idea is to get your colleagues "up and moving."

In a face-to-face professional development session that is approximately one hour in length:

- Place participants in heterogeneous groupings with three to four in each group.
- Give a set of answer cards to each group.
- The groups then go throughout the room and search for the containers. When they find a container, they open it and check to see whether the question in it matches any of their answers. If it does, they take the container and put both the question and the answer in it. If it does not, they return the question to the container.
- At the conclusion of the activity, debrief the session with your colleagues.
- If time allows, ask the groups to unpack at least one of the other Select Response activities and use the Graffiti Wall activity to explore the other strategies.
- Give participants this task: "Use at least one of the Select Response formative assessment techniques in your class over the next week and be ready to discuss how it went." Optional: require participants to try out two of the tasks.

Step 3

Conduct walkthroughs as teachers implement the Select Response formative assessment strategies over the next week. Consider collaborative walkthroughs as well as individual peer walkthroughs.

Step 4

In a follow-up face-to-face professional development session that is approximately one hour in length:

- Ask participants to develop Entrance Tickets and Exit Tickets they believe should be used as a part of a professional development session for other teachers around the Select Response formative assessment strategy. Ask them to reflect on the last session: What would have been good Exit Tickets at the conclusion of that session? What would have been good Entrance Tickets for this session?

- Put participants in groups of four (either heterogeneous or with like grade levels/subject areas). Ask them to discuss their Entrance Tickets and Exit Tickets. Then have the groups share out the results of their discussions.

- Have each group then discuss the following reflection questions:

    - What task did you try? What worked well? What might you do differently next time?

    - What instructional decisions did you make based on the task?

    - How will you use this professional development to make a change in your practice that positively impacts your students and their achievement?

PART

V

Supply Response: Formative Assessment Strategies
Integrating Select Response into Formative Assessments

Supply Response items, also known as *constructed response*, do exactly what they say: they require students to supply information themselves in order to answer a question or prompt. Unlike Select Response, in which the teacher provides a set of predetermined answers from which the student should pick the best choice(s), Supply Response items require that students not simply be able to recognize a correct answer, but either recall it from memory or provide a more in-depth answer using reasoning and/ or creativity.

Like all types of formative assessment strategies, Supply Response has its advantages and drawbacks. Perhaps the best advantage of a Supply Response formative assessment is that, when the item is created properly, it is much more difficult for a student to produce a correct answer simply through guessing. The teacher can generally be assured that if a student answers the question or prompt in a correct fashion, the student actually knows and/or understands the standard being assessed. Supply Response items also allow teachers to assess standards that are written at higher levels—indeed, Supply Response items can assess standards all the way up to the Create level.

It is this ability to assess standards at the higher level that has encouraged a rise in popularity of Supply Response items on assessments, including standardized assessments. Unfortunately, due to the emphasis on Select Response items in the past, teachers have often been slow to adopt more Supply Response items in their classrooms, often to leading to students struggling with these types of items on standardized assessments. There-fore, another happy consequence of using more Supply Response items in the classroom is that in addition to being able to have a more accurate picture of students' abilities to process at higher levels, the use of these types of items can also lead to a rise in standardized assessment scores (Tankersley, 2007).

Another helpful aspect of the Supply Response formative assessment is that it can be used not only to determine *what* students know, but what they *think about* what they know. For instance, a teacher might not only ask students to respond to a prompt but also how comfortable they feel in their knowledge, or what questions they still have about the topic. Moreover, Supply Response items often allow the teacher to determine the *extent* to which a student knows or understands the required information, and to assess other skills as well, such as the student's ability to think critically. Lastly, Supply Response items can allow students some flexibility and creativity, which can lead to greater engagement.

Of course, this flexibility in the way in which students can answer a Supply Response prompt or question is a disadvantage as well. Unlike Select Response items, which can be graded quickly and with little subjectivity, Supply Response items may take longer to grade and require more analysis on the part of the teacher. It is recommended that before grading, the teacher consider what he or she is looking for specifically in the answers (for instance, that the student remembers specific information or can attack the prompt with a certain level of critical thinking) in order to be able to making meaning of the responses and use the information to inform instruction more quickly.

Tips for Using Supply Response Tasks for Formative Assessment

● When developing a Supply Response assessment, consider how long you want students to take on the task. Use that information to influence the design of the questions or prompts and make sure you communicate to students how long they will have to complete the work. Because many of these types of assessments allow students to be creative and think critically, they can unintentionally end up taking too much time during the lesson if not designed and communicated properly.

- It might be necessary to model how to complete the Supply Response item to students, especially if it is in a format that they have never seen before. Teachers might also consider using gradual release to have students complete the item, allowing students to work with a partner the first time they respond to a Supply Response item.

Assessment

3–2–1

Description

The 3–2–1 is a versatile formative assessment that works best when used after students have learned new information (as opposed to a pre-assessment). The teacher asks students to respond to three prompts, like so:

- What are three new things you learned today?
- What are two questions you still have about the topic?
- What is one thing you enjoyed about the lesson?

The teacher can also change the prompts, however, as seen in the "Examples by Subject" section.

Category of Cognitive Process Dimension

Because the teacher is asking students to sum up their learning in a very general way, this task works well for all categories.

Learning Management

The teacher will need to determine ahead of time whether students should work on their own or can do a think-pair-share before filling out the 3–2–1.

Using the Data Effectively

The teacher should examine common themes about the new things learned that day. If a majority of the students does not describe important takeaways from the lesson, the teacher may want to review them with the whole class.

If there are common questions, the teacher will want to address them with the whole class. Otherwise, the teacher will want to follow up with individual students regarding their questions.

Lastly, the teacher will want to use the information about what students enjoyed in order to plan upcoming instruction.

Modifying and Differentiating the Strategy

Students who are not strong writers can complete their 3–2–1 orally. Younger students might be asked only one or two of the prompts, or asked to give fewer examples of things they learned and questions they still have.

Examples by Subject

These examples are questions that could be used for the various subject areas.

English Language Arts

After a lesson on persuasive essays:

- What are three things you learned today about writing effective persuasive essays?
- What are two questions you still have?
- What is one way you can see yourself using persuasive essays in the future?

Mathematics

After a lesson on graphing:

● What are three types of graphs we learned about and what are they used for?

● What are two questions you still have on graphing?

● Which one is your favorite graph and why?

Science

After a lesson on using scientific inquiry to test sound waves:

● What are three things you learned about sound waves after this lesson?

● What are two questions you still have?

● What is one thing you enjoyed about today's lesson?

Social Studies

After a lesson on behaviorist versus cognitive psychology in a Psychology class:

● What are three ways that behaviorist and cognitive psychology are different?

● What are two questions that you still have?

● Which one do you tend to agree with more: the behaviorist or cognitive perspective? Why?

World Languages

After a lesson on mealtime customs in Spain:

● What are three ways that mealtime customs in Spain are similar to many American mealtime customs?

- What are two ways that they are different?
- What is one mealtime custom in Spain that you wish was common in America?

Music

After a lesson on the blues styles in Jazz Band:

- What are three ways that the blues differ from classical music?
- What two things do you need to work on after our performances today?
- What is one question that you still have?

Visual Arts

After a lesson on the Impressionists:

- What are three characteristics of the Impressionist style?
- Name two reactions of critics to the Impressionists during the 1870s and 1880s.
- Which one Impressionist painting or artist speaks to you the most? Why?

Health/Physical Education

After a second-grade lesson on lawn and target games:

- What are three games that you can play with your family in your backyard or at a park that use targets?
- Which two games would you most enjoy playing?
- What is one good strategy to help you do well in a target game?

Library/Media

After a lesson on the AGOPPE (Ask questions, Gather information, Organize information, Prepare, Present, Evaluate) research model:

- What are three major takeaways for you from today's lesson?
- What are two questions that you still have?
- What is one thing that you enjoyed about today's lesson?

Career and Technical Education

After an Inventions and Innovations lesson on significant inventions throughout human history:

- What are three qualities often held by some of the most significant inventions in human history?
- What two inventions do you feel have made the biggest impact on human civilization?
- What is one future invention that you think will have a similarly significant impact on human history?

The Task from Start to Finish

Identify

Marc Blankenship teaches eighth-grade Art and is working with his students on using monochromatic color schemes to create atmosphere. He specifically is working with his students on using a blue color palette to create winter scenes.

Plan

Marc reviews his district's Art standards for this unit, which include the following:

Students will be able to employ a monochromatic color scheme to express emotion or create atmosphere in two-dimensional art.

Phrase	Cognitive Process Dimension Category	Reasoning
Students will be able to employ a monochromatic color scheme to express emotion or create atmosphere in original works of two-dimensional art.	Create	Although "employ" suggests the Apply level, ultimately what students are doing is using the technique to create a work of original art, and the standard is therefore at the Create level.

Apply

Marc reviews Picasso's blue period with the students as an example of how to use a blue color palette to express emotion. He reviews the "cool" side of the color wheel to help students understand the types of colors they will want to use in their original works of a winter scene. He then demonstrates to students how to sketch a winter scene and use lights and darks for contrast. After his students create their own sketches, he shows them how to shade in values using light and dark tones.

While students work, Marc provides feedback to students on their technique and keeps informal notes on their progress using a rubric he has created for monochromatic two-dimensional art. He also wants to know what the students think about their own progress, however, so halfway through their winter scene pieces, he gives them the following 3–2–1 activity with the following prompts:

- What are three techniques you are using to create atmosphere for your winter scene?
- What are two questions you have or difficulties you've found while using a monochromatic color palette?

● What is one way you can see yourself using a monochromatic color palette in future works?

Assess

Marc reviews his students' 3–2–1 slips individually and makes notes. Here is an example:

Name: Deonte
What are three techniques you are using to create atmosphere for your winter scene?

Choosing blue and blue-violets

Using some black and gray

Blending and shading

What are two questions you have or difficulties you've found while using a monochromatic color palette?

The whole thing feels really dark and heavy, which is not how I feel during the winter.

I think I prefer contrasting colors.

What is one way you can see yourself using a monochromatic color palette in future works?

I can see all blue being useful especially to show that someone is sad.

Sure enough, Marc notices that Deonte's work evokes a feeling of heaviness throughout. Marc had assumed Deonte had done this purposefully, but from the 3–2–1 task, he understands otherwise. He also notices four other students say something similar in their 3–2–1, so Marc asks the class about it the next day, and it leads to a lesson on how to use less black and dark gray so they do not compete with the blues, and how to use white to lift out the lightest lights.

Refine

Marc found the 3–2–1 helpful in order to assess his students' thoughts on their own understandings. He decides in addition to providing feedback on student work, he will also do these periodic checks to see what students think about what they're doing. Marc has frequently had students complete critiques after they have finished a piece, but has also found it helpful to formatively assess students' thoughts while they are working so that he can further help them to express their ideas successfully.

Assessment

18

I Think/I Wonder

Description

This is a very simple formative assessment task that works best after a chunk of learning, such as at the end of the teacher explanation portion of the lesson or the end of the lesson itself. In addition to formatively assessing what students know, it can also be used to facilitate classroom discussion.

The teacher hands each student a notecard or scrap of paper. On the front, the student writes the "I think" statement that describes what they think is the major takeaway from the learning. On the back, they write an "I wonder" statement, which is one question they have about the learning.

The question can be a clarifying question (e.g., "What do telomeres do in the cell?"), an opinion question ("Which character in Jane Eyre would you most want to invite to dinner?") or a procedural question ("Are we allowed to turn in a rough draft for feedback before we turn in the final draft?")

This task can either facilitate conversations for the whole group or in small groups. The teacher determines which student will go first and gives that student the direction to read his or her question or comment. The second student then has two different ways to respond: (1) respond to the first person's statement or question; or (2) share her or his own question or statement. The third person to go can similarly either respond to either of the first two people's questions/statements or share his or her own question/statement. This task works especially well for students who are reluctant to participate in or unused to classroom discussions because it scaffolds the participation for them.

The teacher should collect the cards at the end of the learning period and use the data to determine student major takeaways and also address any clarifying or procedural questions that students may have.

Category of Cognitive Process Dimension

This task can work for every cognitive category, from Remember through Create, because students sum up their learning in the classroom.

Learning Management

The teacher will need to model for students how to sum up their learning and the three types of questions. For students who have never participated in a classroom discussion before, the teacher will also want to model to students how to engage in a discussion effectively.

The teacher can either address clarifying or procedural questions immediately or address them soon after the learning takes place (later that day or in the beginning of the next block). It is important for the teacher to actually address the questions to build trust with students.

Using the Data Effectively

After students complete their I Think/I Wonder, teachers should review what they write and address any misconceptions. Teachers can either work with individual students based on their misunderstandings or look for misconception themes and address them with the whole class.

Modifying and Differentiating the Strategy

Students who are not strong writers can draw pictures and orally explain them rather than writing in complete sentences.

Examples by Subject

English Language Arts

Students may use I Think/I Wonder to sum up information from a piece of text or share their thoughts about the writing process for a particular assignment.

Mathematics

Students can share their understanding of a new formula or the problem-solving process.

Science

I Think/I Wonder can be used both to determine student understanding of scientific concepts, and to sum up work with experiments, simulations, or other hands-on learning.

Social Studies

The teacher can have students sum up their understanding of historical events, geographic regions, psychological principles, and more.

World Languages

Major cultural understandings, grammatical usage, and takeaways from works of literature in the language being studied are all potential examples of how this strategy can be used.

Music

Students can use I Think/I Wonder to sum up their understanding of musical theory concepts, instrumental or vocal techniques, or time periods in music.

Visual Arts

The teacher can have students share their takeaways after working on a particular project as a method of reflecting on their own work.

Health/Physical Education

Students can sum up their thoughts on their performance during a particular physical exercise or describe their learning about major health topics.

Library/Media

The teacher can use I Think/I Wonder to have students share their learning from an inquiry project and ask questions for future inquiry.

Career and Technical Education

I Think/I Wonder can be used to assess student understanding of a wide variety of topics, from childcare to culinary arts to automotive repair.

The Task from Start to Finish

Identify

Darby Pterkowsi teaches 12th-grade Government. She is teaching a unit on local, state, and national elections and her particular lesson today is on gerrymandering, or redrawing political boundaries in order to benefit one group's political influence over another.

Plan

Darby reviews the National Curriculum Standards for Social Studies, and unpacks the Power, Authority, and Governance standard:

Process: Learners will be able to analyze and evaluate conditions, actions, and motivations that contribute to conflict and cooperation among groups and nations.

Phrase	Cognitive Process Dimension Category	Reasoning
Learners will be able to analyze and evaluate conditions, actions, and motivations that contribute to conflict and cooperation among groups and nations.	Analyze, Evaluate	In order to work at the appropriate level, students will need to not only compare/contrast the conditions, actions, and motivations that contribute to conflict and cooperation among groups and nations but also evaluate all those concepts by making decisions based on evidence.

Apply

During the lesson Darby goes through an exercise with her students in which she tells them they need to sort themselves according to the shirt color they are wearing and sit in a seat at her five tables. She will then give each table one "vote" about which color shirt should get to go to lunch five minutes early; whichever color gets the most votes from the five tables wins.

The catch is only a student who is wearing the same color shirt as the majority of the students at that table will get to vote for which shirt color will go to lunch five minutes early.

Throughout the course of the activity, students wearing black shirts are in the majority and figure out how to distribute themselves so that they dominate three of the five of the tables. When Darby calls on a person in a black shirt from each table to vote, they all vote for black shirts to go to lunch early, much to the dismay of the rest of the class.

Darby then has students read a passage on gerrymandering and work together in groups of three to explain how this lesson was similar to the gerrymandering that takes place in state elections. At the end of the lesson, Darby has students fill out an "I Think/I Wonder" card and uses it to facilitate a class discussion. She answers clarifying and procedural questions at the beginning of the next class.

Assess

Darby collects all of the cards as students leave so that she can review them. Below are three examples and what Darby concludes from them.

Trinity

I think this lesson shows how gerrymandering is terrible and should be illegal. What if the cafeteria is out of nachos by the time I get there? I hate hot dogs.	I wonder why no one has made gerrymandering illegal.

Jasson

I think this lesson relates to the gerrymandering that happens in our elections. It's hard to stop gerrymandering because the people in power want to stay there and won't change the laws if it doesn't benefit them.	I wonder how we can get more people to vote and potentially help end gerrymandering.

Felicia

I think this lesson is important for all Americans to understand how politicians "stack the deck" so that their party can stay in power. It makes it look like the majority of people believe one thing, but in many cases, the party in power has just redistributed the votes.	I wonder how if an introduction of a popular third party to the major two-party system would help disrupt the system of gerrymandering.

What Darby sees here is a scale from least to most sophisticated. Trinity's major takeaway, for instance, seems to center around cafeteria food. Similarly, her "I wonder" shows a lack of in-depth understanding the process of gerrymandering is legal because it tends to benefit those who are in power by keeping them in power. Jasson, however, has a more sophisticated takeaway; he does understand the causes of gerrymandering and barriers to resolving it. His "I Wonder" also comes up with a potential solution. Felicia's takeaway similarly shows more sophistication and understanding of the intricacy of the issue, and her "I Wonder" shows an even more nuanced understanding of the relationship between the two-party system and gerrymandering.

Darby uses the information to group students for her project-based learning activity for the next week, ensuring that in each group there is someone with a more nuanced understanding of the topic in each group.

Refine

Darby realizes when she reviews the students' cards the next morning that some of them had questions about their homework assignments. Darby decides next time, she will answer questions either immediately or by contacting students digitally that evening to answer the questions.

19 | Sample Student Scenario

Description

The teacher gives students a sample problem completed by an example student (it can be a fictional student) with a common error. In journals or on a half-sheet of paper, ask students to identify the error and explain to the example student in a sentence or a paragraph how to fix it (as appropriate for the level of the problem and the students).

Category of Cognitive Process Dimension

This task can be used for any cognitive category from Remember to Evaluate, but is itself at the Evaluate level. Once students become used to this kind of exercise, the teacher can invite students to make their own Sample Student Scenario, therefore raising it to the Create level.

Learning Management

If you do use an actual student's work, make sure to remove any identifying characteristics, such as the name. If using a student's written work, retype it (including any mistakes you want corrected) or copy it in your own handwriting. Make sure to emphasize this is not about pointing out mistakes, but about learning how to grow and improve.

Using the Data Effectively

The teacher can use the information to quickly see who does and does not understand the concepts being studied in order to act upon that information. For instance, the teacher could easily identify which students understand the basic concepts and know how to justify their thinking.

The teacher could implement this at the beginning or end of a unit or lesson (or both!) and use the information to determine prior student knowledge and whether skills from previous learning need to be retaught before starting the unit lesson.

Modifying and Differentiating the Strategy

For young students or those who have never engaged in this type of exercise before, it might be necessary for the teacher to model how to think through this task answering before asking students to complete it independently. Additionally, the teacher might also have students explain their thinking to a partner before writing their response.

In some cases, the teacher might have students simply discuss the answer rather than writing it down. When possible, it is preferred that the teacher ensures that all students interact with the Sample Student Scenario—having them write individually is one particularly effective way of making sure that everyone participates. The teacher can also read the scenario aloud to struggling readers. If the classroom has a high climate of trust and experience working with this task, the teacher can also move to having students peer-review each other's work in a similar fashion.

Examples by Subject

These examples are prompts that could be used for the various subject areas.

English Language Arts

Jeremiah writes the following sentence: "Their going to the store later too."
Write the sentence correctly. Then use one to three sentences to explain to Jeremiah WHY you made these edits.

Mathematics

Frida's teacher gives her the following problem: There are 20 chairs that need to be arranged into 4 rows. How many chairs will be in each row? Frida answers "16."

In about a paragraph, tell Frida what error she made. Then explain to her how to find the correct answer.

Science

Claudia wants to know what type of fertilizer works best on marigolds. She has three marigold plants. She places each on the same windowpane and gives them the same amount of water each day. On Plant A, she uses Fertilizer A; on Plant B, she uses Fertilizer B; and on Plant C, she uses Fertilizer C. She measures each plant every day, and at the end of the trial period, concludes that Fertilizer A works the best.

In a paragraph, explain to Claudia how she could make this experiment more rigorous.

Social Studies

Riley writes a paper in which he explains that the main cause of the Civil War was desire for freedom from Great Britain.

Pretend you are speaking to Riley. Explain his error—and the real reason(s) for the war.

World Languages

Kelli states to a classmate: "Je parlez le Français."

Write the sentence correctly. Then use one to three sentences to explain to Kelli WHY you made these edits.

Music

Franklin plays several bars of a piece of music incorrectly. Look at the sheet music while I play Franklin's version. [Teacher plays music].

Identify on a notecard how the piece was played incorrectly and then play it correctly with a partner.

Visual Arts

Chenile identifies Munch's *The Scream* as an Impressionist painting.

In one paragraph, correctly identify the artistic movement to which *The Scream* belongs, and explain Chenile's error to her.

Health/Physical Education

Ruben wants to engage in cardiovascular exercise, so he starts a gym membership and lifts free-weights there twice a week.

In a list of three to five bullet points, outline three to five strategies Ruben could do to more effectively achieve his goal.

Library/Media

Keyron is looking for the book *One Fish, Two Fish, Red Fish, Blue Fish* by Dr. Seuss. He looks on the 590 shelves for Animals, but he cannot find the book. Explain to Keyron why his searches haven't led him to the book and how he can find it.

Career and Technical Education

Maria is creating a business plan to market the personalized smartphone covers she creates.

Read her business plan and make three to five suggestions about how she can improve it.

The Task from Start to Finish

Identify

Cora McRoberts teaches fourth grade and is about to start a unit on fractions. From her school's standardized assessment data from the previous year, she knows that fractions were a difficult skill for her students, and the unit will require strong formative assessment.

Plan

Cora reviews the Common Core Mathematics standards, and finds one that has been particularly tricky for students:

CCSS.MATH.CONTENT.4.NF.A.2. Compare two fractions with different numerators and different denominators, e.g., by creating common denominators or numerators, or by comparing to a benchmark fraction such as $\frac{1}{2}$. Recognize comparisons are valid only when the two fractions refer to the same whole. Record the results of comparisons with symbols >, =, or <, and justify the conclusions, e.g., by using a visual fraction model.

Phrase	Cognitive Process Dimension Category	Reasoning
Compare two fractions with different numerators and different denominators, e.g., by creating common denominators or numerators, or by comparing to a benchmark fraction such as $\frac{1}{2}$.	Apply	Students are using a procedure to carry out the task of comparing fractions with different numerators and different denominators. Even though the word create is in this sentence, this does not truly meet the definition of Create as it is used in Bloom's Revised Taxonomy. Because students are "creating" new common denominators or numerators in order to compare the fractions, it is really the Apply level (changing to common denominators or numerators) in order to Analyze (comparing the fractions).

Recognize that comparisons are valid only when the two fractions refer to the same whole.	Understand	In this case, the word *recognize* is used to show that students understand the concept that they have to change two dissimilar fractions so that they refer to the same whole in order to compare them.
Record the results of comparisons with symbols >, =, or <, and justify the conclusions, e.g., by using a visual fraction model.	Apply Evaluate	When students "record the results," it implies that they are solving the problem—which is the Apply level. When they "justify the conclusions," they are working at the Evaluate level to explain why their answer is correct using evidence.

After unpacking this standard and determining her students need to work at several levels from Understand through Evaluate, Cora decides the Sample Student Scenario task would be a great way to gather information about whether her students can work at all these levels. More than just having students answer a problem, it will allow her to see if students can understand fractional number sense on a deep level—instead of just following steps to solve an equation.

Apply

Cora creates the task for students by developing this prompt:

Jose's teacher asks him to compare $\frac{3}{8}$ and $\frac{2}{5}$. Jose turns in this answer:

$\frac{3}{8} > \frac{2}{5}$ because there are 3 of the eighths and only 2 of the fifths and 5 is less than 8.

UNDERSTAND: Jose's teacher asks you to work with him to explain to him WHY this answer is incorrect by doing the following in a paragraph below:

APPLY: Solve the problem correctly yourself.

EVALUATE: Draw a picture that explains to Jose how you know your solution is correct.

Because this is only the third time that students have engaged in this task, and because fractions are often a difficult concept for fourth graders, Cora reads the task aloud to all students, and then lets her students work in pairs beforehand and use manipulatives to scaffold their thinking while she monitors and provides feedback as necessary. After 15 minutes, she then has students work independently for another 15 minutes to write out their answers. For two of her students with writing disabilities, she pulls them to a corner of the room and has them explain their answers to her. Cora scripts their answers to ensure that their writing ability does not cause issues with the validity of the assessment but allows the students to draw the pictures themselves.

Assess

After students complete the assignment, Cora marks on a clean sheet of the assignment who does not adequately answer each section, like this:

Jose's teacher asks him to compare and Jose turns in this answer:

because there are 2 of the fifths and only 1 of the fourths.

UNDERSTAND: Jose's teacher asks you to work with him to explain to him WHY this answer is incorrect by doing the following in a paragraph below:
INCORRECT: Tasha, Everett, Jane, Michael, June, Jamison, LaVon, Maria, Chelsea

APPLY: Solve the problem correctly yourself:
INCORRECT: Jane, Michael, LaVon, Maria

EVALUATE: Draw a picture that explains to Jose how you know your solution is correct:
INCORRECT: Everett, Jane, Michael, June, Jamison, Lavon, Maria

---

Based on this example, Cora decides for her math groups the next day she will need to see Jane, Michael, Lavon, and Maria in one group, and review basic number sense with fractions using manipulatives. She will also need to review the computation of how to actually compare fractions with these students.

Everett, June, Jamison do not appear to understand either how to explain why the sample student's answer was incorrect, nor how to draw the solution—but they do seem to know the computation. Even though Tasha and Chelsea were able to correctly draw a problem, she decides to group them with Everett, June, and Jamison to review how to communicate their mathematical reasoning, possibly keeping Everett, June, and Jamison for an extra five minutes to review drawing representations of fractions.

While she works with these students in small groups, Cora decides to group the other students who "got it" and allow them to create their own word problems similar to the "Jose" scenario, as well as have them test each other to find the errors.

Refine

Cora reviews the Sample Student Scenario that she gave to students. Upon remediation, two of her students, Tasha and Chelsea, were easily able to explain their thinking; both reported that they just weren't sure how they were supposed to answer the question. Two of Cora's teammates report a portion of their students had similar problems with answering the prompt. They and Cora decide before she uses this task next time, she will once again model how to answer this type of prompt for the whole class.

Would You Rather

Description

This takes a simple task (asking someone to choose between two concepts) and turns it into a fun formative assessment. The teacher presents two choices (e.g., "Would you rather meet President Washington or President Lincoln?") and asks students to choose and explain why. Answers can be written or presented orally. The teacher then determines levels of student understanding based on their responses.

It is up to the teacher whether to use a Would You Rather question with a correct answer. If the question has a correct answer, the teacher can use the information to better pinpoint whether students have an accurate understanding of the content. If the question does not have a correct answer, students might feel less intimidated to answer honestly and creatively, yielding a wider range of information about student understanding.

Category of Cognitive Process Dimension

The task itself has students working within the Evaluate category, because it requires them to make a decision and base it on evidence. The task can work with any standards up to the Evaluate level.

Learning Management

It is helpful to model to students how you want them to provide evidence so that they do not simply pick one of the choices.

Using the Data Effectively

A teacher can divide students quickly based upon both content knowledge and critical thinking/sophistication of the justification.

 # Modifying and Differentiating the Strategy

Students who are not strong writers can give their answers orally. The teacher can also use this as a think-pair-share and to start a classroom discussion.

Examples by Subject

These examples are questions that could be used for the various subject areas.

English Language Arts

"Would you rather go to dinner with Heathcliff or Edgar Linton from *Wuthering Heights?*"

Mathematics

"Would you rather have a job where your hourly wage is twice as much as your age plus 12 years—or a job where your hourly wage is three times as much as your age plus two years?"

Science

"Would you rather be an herbivore or a carnivore?"

Social Studies

"Would you be a reporter investigating Tammany boss William M. Tweed, or a reporter investigating the Teapot Dome Scandal?"

World Languages

"Would you rather visit Spain or Costa Rica in December?"

Music

"Would you rather perform a piece of music written by Mozart in front of Mozart, or a piece of music written by Beethoven in front of Beethoven?"

Visual Arts

"Would you rather train with Monet or Picasso?"

Health/Physical Education

"Would you rather do an hour of yoga or jog for an hour?"

Library/Media

"If you saw your friend being cyber-bullied, would you rather confront the student doing the bullying, or tell an adult?"

Career and Technical Education

(Economics and Personal Finance:) "Would you rather put $1,000 in a high-risk investment with a greater potential payout, or put it in a low-risk investment with a guaranteed low payout?"

The Task from Start to Finish

Identify

Ethelyn Parks teaches first-grade students. She has been working with her students on comparing two-digit numbers. Ethelyn has been using the Concrete-Representational-Abstract method with her students (also known as the CRA method). She started all her students using base-10 blocks to build and compare the numbers; as individual students were ready (Concrete stage), she had them move on to drawing representations of the numbers to compare (Representational stage). Again, as individual students mastered the Representational stage, she moved them to the Abstract stage, where she would give them just numerals to compare.

Ethelyn has not yet introduced the concept of >, =, or < signs yet, and wants to know who in her class is ready for it. She has been teaching the concept mostly in small groups and is also ready to reorganize her small groups based on student understanding.

Plan

Ethelyn unpacks the following Common Core Mathematics standard:

CCSS.MATH.CONTENT.1.NBT.B.3.   Compare two two-digit numbers based on meanings of the tens and ones digits, recording the results of comparisons with the symbols >, =, and <.

Phrase	Cognitive Process Dimension Category	Reasoning
Compare two two-digit numbers based on meanings of the tens and ones digits, recording the results of comparisons with the symbols >, =, and <.	Understand	Students use the Comparing cognitive process of the Understand level to compare two numbers; they show their understanding of what makes one number "greater than" or "less than" than another.

Apply

Ethelyn pulls students in small groups in order to assess them. She puts up cardboard dividers between students so that she can see what they are doing, but they cannot see each other's work. She gives them the prompt, "Would you rather earn $12 for washing a car, or $21?"

Each student has an individual whiteboard, a dry-erase marker, and base-10 blocks.

Assess

Ethelyn keeps a chart that looks like this during her small groups:

	Solves Concretely	Solves Representationally	Solves Abstractly
Content: Recognizes that $21 is more than $12	Micala (SP) Julie (NP) Quentin (SP) William (SP) Ava (NP)	Noah (NP) Lima (MP) Bennett (MP)	Esme (NP) Shauna (NP) Phillip (NP) Taevon (NP) Garrett (NP) Emma (NP) Harper (NP) Charlotte (NP) Alexander (MP)

NP = No Prompting

MP = Moderate Prompting

SP = Significant Prompting

While watching students work, Ethelyn does "whisper conferences" with them. As students work, she provides prompts for those who need it, and when they select an answer, she will whisper, "How do you know you're right?" so that they can justify their thinking.

What Ethelyn notices is several of her students are ready to move on to the >, =, < symbols. All those who were able to solve concretely, most without prompting. She also notices several students (Noah, Julie, and Ava) were able to answer quickly using either manipulatives or drawn pictures.

She goes back and asks them another problem ("Would you rather be paid $34 or $43 for cleaning a house?") without offering manipulatives or pictures. Julie and Ava both answer easily without the use of manipulatives or pictures; Noah still needs to draw the answer in order to make a determination. She therefore decides that Ava and Julie both are indeed ready to move on to learning the <, =, and > signs.

Refine

Ethelyn see the students enjoy the activity and determines she will use it not just at the end of a lesson, but also as a lesson activity as part of a think-pair-share, so students can continue to practice justifying their thinking with their peers.

Professional Development Plan
Supply Response Tasks

Step 1

Read the chapter in advance of meeting as a group. Ask the participants to bring a lesson they have planned and will teach within the next two weeks.

Step 2

In a face-to-face professional development session that is approximately one hour in length:

- Pair teachers across grade level and cross-content (if possible).

- Ask each teacher to share the lesson she or he has brought and to provide a brief background/context of the lesson, the purpose of the lesson within the larger curriculum framework, and the outcomes for the lesson. Of course, the teacher should also fully explain the lesson to his or her partner. Each teacher should have about 10 minutes to share. Probing questions are encouraged, but the listening partner should refrain from interjecting opinions or suggestions when the other is presenting.

- After each person has shared, ask the teachers to quietly fill out an I Think/I Wonder sheet about her or his partner's lesson. After each person has completed the I Think/I Wonder, allow the teachers to then discuss what they wrote.

- At the conclusion of the activity debrief the session with the participants.

- If time allows, break the participants into groups and ask them to unpack at least one of the other Supply Response activities and to use the Graffiti Wall activity to explore the other strategies.

- Give participants this task: "Use at least one of the Supply Response formative assessment techniques in your class over the next week and be ready to discuss how it went." Optional: require participants to try out two of the tasks.

Step 3

Conduct walkthroughs as staff implement the Supply Response formative assessment strategies over the next week. Consider collaborative walk-throughs as well as individual peer walkthroughs.

Step 4

In a follow-up face-to-face professional development session approxi-mately one hour in length:

- Ask teachers as they enter to answer the following questions on a large (4 × 6) index card.

  - What are three new things you have learned about Supply Response formative assessments?

  - What are two questions you have about the Supply Response for-mative assessments?

  - What is one thing you enjoyed about using the Supply Response formative assessments in your class these past two weeks?

- Put participants in groups of four (either heterogeneous or with like grade levels/subject areas). Ask them to discuss their 3–2–1 index card responses. Encourage discussion with the group at large once the smaller groups have exhausted their discussion points.

- Have each group then discuss the following reflection questions.

- What task did you try? What worked well? What might you do differently next time?
- What instructional decisions did you make based on the task?
- How will you use this professional development to make a change in your practice that positively impacts your students and their achievement?

References

Ackerman, D. S., Dommeyer, C. J., & Gross, B. J. (2016). The effects of source, revision possibility, and amount of feedback on marketing students' impressions on feedback on an assignment. *Journal of Marketing Education, 39*(1), 17–29.

Anderson, L. W. (Ed.), Krathwohl, D. R. (Ed.), Airasian, P. W., Cruikshank, K. A., Mayer, R. E., Pintrich, P. R., . . . Wittrock, M. C. (2001). *A taxonomy for learning, teaching, and assessing: A revision of Bloom's Taxonomy of Educational Objectives* (Complete ed.). New York: Longman.

Armstrong, S. (2008). *Teaching smarter with the brain in focus: Practical ways to apply the latest brain research to deepen comprehension, improve memory, and motivate students to achieve.* New York: Scholastic.

Armstrong, T. (2016). Move with purpose: Four approaches to making content kinesthetic. *ASCD Express: Ideas from the Field, 12*(3).

Asaridou, S. S., & McQueen, J. M. (2013). Speech and music shape the listening brain: Evidence for shared domain-general mechanisms. *Frontiers in Psychology, 4,* 321.

Black, P. (2003). Formative and summative assessment: Can they serve learning together? In collaboration with the King's College London Assessment for Learning Group, C. Harrison, C. Lee, B. Marshall, and D. Wiliams. Paper presented at American Educational Research Association (AERA), 23 April, in Chicago, IL. SIG Classroom Assessment Meeting 52.028. http://www.kcl.ac.uk//depsta/education/hpages/pblack pubs.html.

Black, P. & Wiliam, D. (1998b). Inside the black box: Raising standards through classroom assessment. *PHI Delta Kappan, 80*(2), 139–44.

Davis, E. (2015). *Want kids to pay attention in class? Give them standing desks.* VITAL RECORD: News from Texas A&M Health Science Center. Retrieved from https://vitalrecord.tamhsc.edu/want-kids-to-pay-attention-in-class-give-them-standing-desks/

Gareis, C. R., & Grant, L. W. (2008). *Teacher-made assessments: How to connect curriculum, instruction, and student learning.* Larchmont, NY: Eye on Education.

Garvis, S., & Pendergast, D. (2010). Supporting novice teachers and the arts. *International Journal of Education and the Arts, 11*(8), 1–23.

Goldin-Meadow, S., Kim, S., & Singer, M. (1999). What the teacher's hands tell the student's mind about math. *Journal of Educational Psychology, 91,* 720–30.

Goldin-Meadow, S., Nusbaum, H., Kelly, S. D., & Wagner, S. (2001). Explaining math: gesturing lightens the load. *Psychological Science, 12*(6), 516–522.

Hattie, J. A. (2009). *Visible learning: A synthesis of over 800 meta-analyses relating to achievement.* London: Routledge.

Jensen, E. (2005). *Teaching with the brain in mind* (2nd ed.). ASCD Books. Retrieved from www.ascd.org/publications/books/104013/chapters/Movement-and-Learning.aspx

Johnson, C. Y. (2013). Learn music, be better at math, right? Study finds it's not so. *The Boston Globe.* Retrieved from www.bostonglobe.com/lifestyle/health-wellness/2013/12/11/music-makes-you-smarter-right-actually-doesn-harvard-study-finds-harvard-study-finds-studying-music-doesn-make-you-smarter/OkdbVM6fQR4hryFuKNm9gJ/story.html

Johnson, D. W. & Johnson, R. T. (2009). An educational psychology success story: Social interdependent theory and cooperative learning. *Educational Researcher, 38*(3), p. 365–379.

Johnson, D. W., & Johnson, R. T. (n.d.). An overview of cooperative learning. *International Conference on Cooperative Learning.* Retrieved from www.co-operation.org/what-is-cooperative-learning/

Kraus, N., & Anderson, S. (2015). Beat-keeping ability relates to reading readiness. *The Hearing Journal, 68*(3), 54–56.

Lyding, L., Zambo, D., & Hansen, C. C. (2014). Move it or lose it. *Educational Leadership, 72*(2). Retrieved from www.ascd.org/publications/educational-leadership/oct14/vol72/num02/Move-It-or-Lose-it!.aspx

McMullen, E. & Saffran, J. R. (2004). Music and language: A developmental comparison. *Music Perception: An interdisciplinary Journal, 21*(3), p. 289–311.

Nuthall, G. (2007). The hidden lives of of learners. Wellington: New Zealand Council for Educational Research Press.

Oreck, B. (2004). The artistic and professional development of teachers: A study of teachers' attitudes toward and use of the arts in teaching. *Journal of Teacher Education, 55*, 55–69.

Otero, V. K. (2006). Moving Beyond the "Get it or Don't" Conception of Formative Assessment. *Journal of Teacher Education, 57*(3), 247–255.

Patel, A. (2003). Language, music, syntax and the brain. *Nature Neuroscience, 6*(7), 674–681.

Pitler, H., Hubbell, E. R., & Kuhn, M. (2012). *Using technology with classroom instruction that works (2nd Ed.)*. Alexandria, VA: ASCD.

Plummer, J. D. (2009). Early elementary students' development of astronomy concepts in the planetarium. *Journal of Research in Science Teaching, 46*(2), 192–209.

Roskos, K., & Neuman, S. B. (2012). Formative assessment: Simply, no additives. *The Reading Teacher, 65*(8), 534–538.

Sanzo, K. S., Myran, S., & Caggiano, J. (2015). *Formative assessment leadership: Identify, plan, apply, assess, refine*. New York, NY: Routledge.

Shoval, E. (2011). Using mindful movement in cooperative learning while learning about angles. *Instructional Science, 39*(4), 453–466.

Silverman, M. J. (2010). The effect of pitch, rhythm, and familiarity on working memory and anxiety as measured by digit recall performance. *Journal of Music Therapy, 47*(1), 70–83.

Slavin, R. E. (2014). Making cooperative learning powerful. *Educational Leadership, 72*(2), 22–26.

Stevens, R. J., & Slavin, R. E. (1990). When cooperative learning improves the achievement of students with mild disabilities: A response to Tateyama-Sniezek. *Exceptional Children, 57*(3), 276–280.

Tankersey, K. (2007). *Tests that teach: Chapter 1. Constructed response: Connecting performance and assessment*. ASCD Books. Retrieved from www.ascd.org/publications/books/107022/chapters/Constructed-Response@-Connecting-Performance-and-Assessment.aspx

Wilhelm, J. (1995). Reading is seeing: Using visual response to improve the literary reading of reluctant readers. *Journal of Reading Behavior, 27*(4), 467–503.

Wilson, L. O. (2016). Anderson and Krathwohl – Bloom's taxonomy revised: Understanding the new version of bloom's taxonomy. http://thesecondprinciple.com/teaching-essentials/beyond-bloom-cognitive-taxonomy-revised/